CW01023166

JAM JAM JAM

with
BON JOVI

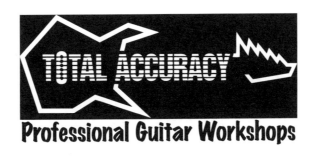

TOTAL ACCURACY
Professional Guitar Workshops

Exclusive Distributors:
Music Sales Limited
8/9 Frith Street
London W1V 5TZ England

Music Sales Pty Limited
120 Rothschild Avenue
Rosebery, NSW 2018
Australia

Order No AM 953931 Jam with Bon Jovi ISBN 0-7119-7197-8
This book © Copyright 1998 by Wise Publications

Unauthorised reproduction of any part of this publication by any means including photocopying is an infringement of copyright.

Printed in Malta by Interprint Limited

Your Guarantee of Quality
As publishers we strive to produce every book to the highest commercial standards. The music has been freshly engraved and the book has been carefully designed to minimise awkward page turns and to make playing from it a real pleasure. Particular care has been given to specifying acid-free, neutral-sized paper made from pulps which have not been elemental chlorine bleached. This pulp is from farmed sustainable forests and was produced with special regard for the environment.
Throughout, the printing and binding have been planned to ensure a sturdy, attractive publication which should give years of enjoyment. If your copy fails to meet our high standards, please inform us and we will gladly replace it.

Music Sales' complete catalogue describes thousands of titles and is available in full colour sections by subject, direct from Music Sales Limited. Please state your areas of interest and send a cheque/postal order for £1.50 for postage to: Music Sales Limited, Newmarket Road, Bury St Edmunds, Suffolk IP33 3YD.

Wise Publications
London/New York/Sydney/Paris/Copenhagen/Madrid

CONTENTS

ON THE CD

The CD is split into two sections; section 1 (tracks 1-8) is the backing tracks minus lead guitar & vocals, while section 2 (tracks 9-16) is the backing tracks with all guitar parts added, so in addition to the written tab you can hear the rhythm, fills and solos as they should be played!! Because of the audio time limitations on a CD some of the tracks in section 2 have had to be edited, although wherever possible we have included the complete track.

Music arranged and produced by Stuart Bull and Steve Finch.
Recorded at the TOTAL ACCURACY SOUNDHOUSE, Romford, England.
Stuart Bull: guitar on tracks 9, 10 & 14.   Jamie Humphries: guitar on tracks 11, 12, 13, 15 & 16.
Mick Ash: bass.   Pete Adams: keyboards.   Pete Riley: drums.
Jamie Humphries uses Ernie Ball Music Man Guitars.

Music transcribed by Guthrie Govan

Cover Design by Kim Waller
Music engraved by Cambridge Notation

Visit the Total Accuracy
Audio Visual Experience at
http://www.totalaccuracy.co.uk

Introduction

THE TOTAL ACCURACY 'JAM WITH...' series is a powerful learning tool that will help you extend your stockpile of licks and fills and develop your improvisational skills. The combination of musical notation and guitar tablature in the book, together with backing tracks on the CD, gives you the opportunity to learn each track note for note and then jam with a professional session band. The track listing reflects some of Bon Jovi's most popular recordings, providing something for guitarists to have fun with and improvise with, as well as something to aspire to.

The first eight tracks on the CD are full length backing tracks recorded minus lead guitar. The remaining tracks feature the backing tracks with the lead guitar parts added. Although many of you will have all the original tracks in your own collections, we have provided them in the package for your reference. The 'JAM WITH...' series allows you to accurately recreate the original, or to use the transcriptions in this book in conjunction with the backing tracks as a basis for your own improvisation. For your benefit we have put definite endings on the backing tracks, rather than fading them out as is the case on some of the original recordings. The accompanying transcriptions correspond to our versions. Remember, experimenting with your own ideas is equally important for developing your own style; most important of all, however, is that you enjoy JAM with BON JOVI and HAVE FUN!

Bon Jovi, one of the most successful of all commercial hard rock line-ups, were formed in Sayreville, New Jersey, USA, in the spring of 1983, when a certain JOHN FRANCIS BONGIOVI teamed up with keyboardist DAVID BRYAN (born David Rashbaum), drummer TICO TORRES, bassist ALEC JOHN SUCH and guitarist RICHIE SAMBORA.

Bryan and Bon Jovi had met at high school, and had played together in a 10-piece R&B covers outfit called 'Atlantic City Expressway' before relocating to New York, where Jon obtained a job at the Power Station Studio and Bryan commenced studies at the Juilliard School of Music. The rest of the band were already seasoned players when they came together to play in Bon Jovi's line-up (Such had played in Phantom's Opera and Torres had drummed for the Knockouts, whilst Sambora was an established session guitarist), so the sound came together quickly, leading to a recording contract with Polygram in July 1983, and some prestigious support slots - including a Madison Square Gardens gig with ZZ Top.

The band's eponymous debut album (*Bon Jovi*, 1984) led to a headline tour and some more meaty support slots with the Scorpions, Kiss and Whitesnake, but the follow-up (*7,800 Degrees Farenheit* 1985) was not well-received.

However, Bon Jovi's ascent to the uppermost echelons of the scene really occured when their third album, *Slippery When Wet*, became the biggest-selling rock album of 1987, spawning such US hits as *You Give Love A Bad Name* and the classic anthem *Livin' On A Prayer*; following the album's release with 18 months of solid touring (including the headline slot in the European "Monsters of Rock" tour), the band cemented their position as leaders in their field and went on to produce *New Jersey,* which contained hit singles like *I'll Be There For You* and *Bad Medicine*. After another prolonged tour, Bon Jovi went into temporary and well-earned retirement, giving Jon time to appear in his first film *(Young Guns II),* write the soundtrack for it and marry karate champion Dorothea Hurley.

In 1992, the band re-emerged with shorter hairdos and a less "corporate rock" sound, in the form of the album *Keep The Faith*, which proved that Bon Jovi could still write hits! Since then, the group's output has included the compilation, *Cross Road: The Best of Bon Jovi* and the album

These Days, (which marked Such's departure from the band, to be replaced by Hugh McDonald); in addition, Jon Bon Jovi and Richie Sambora have both successfully pursued solo projects, and it doesn't look like they've given up yet!

Playing through this compilation of Bon Jovi's most acclaimed tracks will give you an insight into how the right guitar part can turn a good song into a great one. It will also provide a workout in everything from laidback acoustic rhythm playing to state-of-the-art rock soloing.

Most importantly, though - it'll be fun!

Performance Notes

Livin' On A Prayer

This song, from the *Slippery When Wet* album, was a huge commercial success when it was released as a single at the end of 1986. The guitar parts have been arranged for one guitar, as there are very few places on the track where more than one guitar is audible (bars 55-58 and bars 92-93). As is the case with many of the songs featured in our selection, *Livin' On A Prayer* ends as a fadeout on the original recorded version, so for ease of playing along the "Total Accuracy" version includes an ending typical of what the band would play in a live setting.

The guitar work in this track can be broken down into 3 categories. Firstly, there is the ostinato riff heard in the intro, marked "with distortion and talkbox" in the music - this theme recurs throughout the song. Then, there is the power chord based riffing in the chorus section which follows the basic rhythm of the vocal line. Finally, there is the solo, which uses the Em Pentatonic (E, G, A, B, D) and G major (G, A, B, C, D, E, F#) scales and features fast chromatic picking in bar 93 and "raking" in bars 86 and 90 (which involves dragging the pick across the strings in a single smooth motion). The solo section is modelled on the structure of the chorus, but it is highlighted by 2 extra bars of C at the beginning, and 2 unexpected Em bars at the end. Also beware of the 3/4 bar in bar 97, and note the very effective touch in the following bar, where the chorus modulates up one-and-a-half tones.

This track was probably recorded using a Charvel or Kramer guitar through a Marshall stack. The "talk-box" mentioned earlier is a device popularised by players like Jeff Beck and Peter Frampton, which combines the guitar sound with a vocal signal, giving the notes "vowel" characteristics. You can approximate the effect using a wah-wah, accentuating the treble frequencies where indicated with an accent marking in the music.

Wanted Dead Or Alive

Another track from the *Slippery When Wet* album, *Dead or Alive* originally featured at least 3 guitar parts, but it has been arranged for two here. The first guitar part is for 12-string acoustic, (although a 6-string instrument will also work) and it plays a theme based on 6th intervals from the D Dorian mode (D, E, F, G, A, B, C) in the intro, before the verse and solo, and at the end. The rest of the time, the chords are strummed with a constant 16th-note feel - but note the variations in places like bar 64 (where 32nd notes are introduced) bar 76 (featuring slow "raking") and bars 71 and 79 (where single-note melodies are heard).

The second guitar part is for electric guitar, and it's a combination of rhythm, solos and fills. Use the volume control on your instrument to keep each section at the appropriate level - atmospheric passages like bars 10-12 are less prominent than the actual solo!

The solo itself is based on the Dm pentatonic scale (D, F, G, A, C), and should be played with plenty of 'pick attack', paying attention to the bends in bar 55. Note the "false ending" in bar 60, comprising a 2/4 bar before the crescendo which leads back into the final section.

The acoustic work on this track was probably performed on an Ovation or Guild 12-string, and the electric playing most likely featured a Charvel or Kramer instrument with Marshall amplification.

You Give Love A Bad Name

This track features plenty of power-chord riffing, and the lead playing showcases a variety of modern rock techniques.

The intro melody comes in at bar 5 and is played by gtr 1 (whilst gtr 2 plays the rhythm part later to be heard in the choruses); this features a harmoniser which adds a note one octave above what is played into it. Bars 13-16 introduce the verse figure, which should be muted by leaning the palm of the right hand on the strings, near the bridge; try to add occasional pinched harmonics and pick quite hard for an "aggressive" sound. (This part is doubled on the record, but a very short delay effect will give a similar result).

In the bridge section, note the use of the vibrato bar. In bars 27-28, for instance, the double-stop should be picked once only, and the written rhythm is outlined by "scooping" with the bar.

The solo is based on the Cm pentatonic scale with an added 2nd (C, D, Eb, F, G, Bb), and it features slow "divebombing" with the bar (bars 76-77), sliding octave shapes (bars 78-79, two-handed tapping where the tapped notes are slid rapidly up the fretboard à la Van Halen (bar 80), unison bends (bar 82) and a muted pentatonic idea at the end, which concludes the solo lower down on the guitar's register than is usual.

The original version of this track fades out, so the version on our jam-track features an ending suitable for live performance. Richie Sambora probably used a Charvel or Kramer guitar, Marshall amps and an AMS harmoniser for gtr 1.

Dry County

This 10-minute epic from the *Keep The Faith* album, contains a variety of sections and several different guitar styles; it has been arranged so that gtr 1 plays the rhythm and clean melody parts, while gtr 2 plays the solos.

In bars 7-11, the clean guitar melody is executed using quick precise bends, and the verse accompaniment is heavily ornamented with fills and arpeggiation; the notes should be allowed to ring into one another where possible.

The pre-chorus sections (e.g. bars 41-44) kicks in with the overdrive, and it uses polychords; note the Dm/C can be viewed as Dm7, and Dm/B is equivalent to Bm7b5.

The first solo (bars 85-95) follows the chorus progression, but caps it with an Am-Bb change. It uses the F major pentatonic scale (F, G, A, C, D) and should be played with a "creamy" overdriven sound.

The section in bars 96-176 is marked "double time", which means the beats are counted at twice the speed, for a more "exciting" feel.

The arpeggio figure in bars 96-127 is picked on the original, but it will also work fingerstyle. The fast rock solo played by gtr 2 in bars 128-176 features a trill punctuated by vibrato bar "scooping" (bars 128-129) tremolo-picked octave shapes (bars 152-155) and a tricky alternate-picked scale sequence (bars 166-167), based on the D dorian scale (D, E, F, G, A, B, C).

A long pickscrape in bar 191 leads the song back to its chorus.

This track was probably recorded using one of Richie's signature-series Fender Stratocasters, through Fender or Trace Elliot amps.

In These Arms

This poppy track from the *Keep The Faith* album has been arranged here for two guitars (there are at least three on the original version). Apart from the solo section, gtr 1 has a brighter, less overdriven tone than gtr 2, to allow the chords to resonate clearly. Note how the E-Esus4 motif occurs in both low (bars 1-8) and high (bars 9-24) registers.

During the chorus, gtr 2 maintains a constant rock rhythm using power-chords, and gtr 1 throws in "hooks" such as the low E-string melody in bar 45, the arpeggiated C#m(sus 2) melody in bar 47 and the figure based on a B chord in bar 51.

Note the E/G# polychord in bar 58; this is an unusual voicing of E major, emphasising the "happy" sounding 3rd.

The solo uses the E major pentatonic scale (E, F#, G#, B, C#); this is equivalent to the C#m pentatonic, so much of the solo is played around the IXth position "blues box".

The original tracks fades out, so we've added an ending resolving on the E chord.

The track was most likely recorded using a Richie Sambora signature-series Stratocaster through Fender or Trace Elliot amplifiers.

Blaze Of Glory

Written by Jon Bon Jovi as part of the soundtrack for the film *Young Guns II*, this song can be found on the album *Blaze of Glory*. Whereas all the other guitar work in this compilation was performed by Richie Sambora, this track features a solo by the mighty Jeff Beck, with all other guitar parts played by Aldo Nova.

The track shares a Western theme and a D minor/D major ambiguity with the track *Dead or Alive*, and it features 4 or 5 guitar tracks on the original version, some in standard tuning (E, A, D, G, B, E) some in drop-D tuning (D, A, D, G, B, E) and some in open D (D, A, D, F#, A, D). Here, it has been arranged for 2 guitars, both in drop-D; gtr 1 is an electric part covering the solo and heavier riffs and gtr 2 is for acoustic, being a combination of strummed rhythm, arpeggiated chords and slide work (for further experimenting, try tuning your acoustic to open D for the slide work).

During the chorus, gtr 2 has been transcribed as a series of slide fills, but it could also play a strummed rhythm part in the same vein as the verse.

The solo features a mixture of slide playing and fretted notes, with some vibrato bar work. Work on muting unwanted strings when playing slide, and try the Jeff Beck technique of executing all the notes fingerstyle, for more attack and control. This solo is a good exercise for your intonation; note that if your vibrato bar cannot raise the pitch of the harmonic in bar 71 by 1&1/2 tones you can play the note on the top E string, using the slide to raise the pitch up to an imaginary 25th fret (over the neck pick-up).

The electric work on this track was played on a Fender Stratocaster through Marshall or Fender amps, and the acoustic work features, a standard flat-top acoustic and also a Dobro-style resonator guitar.

Keep The Faith

Taken from the album of the same name, this track shows a funkier side to the band's music. It has been arranged for two guitars, and the effects marked in the music (tremolo for gtr 1, flanging for gtr 2) are optional.

Starting with some volume-knob swells on the progression G5-G7sus4-G5, the guitar moves into the funky 16th-note feel which characterises the whole song around bar 24. This feel pervades the high-strings-based work in the verse, the octaves in the chorus (gtr 2) and the single notes in the breakdowns (bars 41-44 and 77-84).

The solo is based on the G blues scale (G, Bb, C, Db, D, F) and emphasises the b5 note. This section has a loose feel with occasional double stops, and the main points to watch our for are the shifts between the 1st and 3rd positions, and also the angular-sounding line in bar 88.

Note that the melody at the end (starting in bar 109) is played first by gtr 1, and then "taken over" by gtr 2 an octave higher, to create a build-up effect.

The original track fades out at the end, so we've provided a typical "live-ending" for our arrangement.

The song was probably recorded using a Fender Stratocaster through Fender or Trace Elliot amps, with a Zoom effects unit.

Bad Medicine

The original version of this track can be heard on the *New Jersey* album and it features a single guitar track throughout, with the exception of the solo section which contains both rhythm and lead parts.

The intro/chorus riff makes good use of alternating between the low and high registers of an open E chord - note how the rhythm compliments the vocal line.

The verse sections, (bars 17-29 and 51-59) should be played fingerstyle, using a wah-wah pedal set constantly in the middle of its range, to add a Michael Schenker-esque "honk" to the sound. (A similar sound is heard in the Dire Straits track, *Money for Nothing*).

There are various applications of the vibrato bar throughout. For the "gargles" in bars 50 and 83, pull the bar up a little and suddenly release it, so it "quivers" before returning to pitch. In bar 84, the trem is used to add wide vibrato to natural harmonics, and for the sound effects in bars 89-90, the right hand produces random pinched harmonics from the open strings, while the left hand reaches over to "dab" the bar, so the pitch lowers and immediately returns. The rest of the solo uses the Em pentatonic scale (E,G, A, B, D) with the fast alternate picking section in bar 92 combining the E dorian scale (E, F#, G, A, B, C#, D) with some chromatic notes (F♮, G#, Bb, D#).

Other points of note here include the octave figure in bars 123-124, which is emphasised by the bass and drums, and the "false-ending" around bar 129, featuring a 2/4 bar before returning at bar 132 to play through the chorus (in the words of Jon) "One more time with feeling!".

This track was probably performed on a Kramer guitar with a Marshall amp.

Notation & Tablature Explained

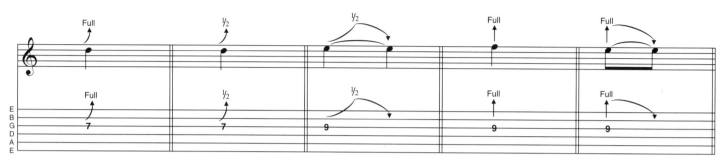

BEND: Strike the note and bend up a whole step (two frets).

BEND: Strike the note and bend up a half step (one fret).

BEND AND RELEASE: Strike the note, bend up a half step, then release the bend.

PRE-BEND: Bend the note up, then strike it.

PRE-BEND AND RELEASE: Bend up, strike the note, then release it.

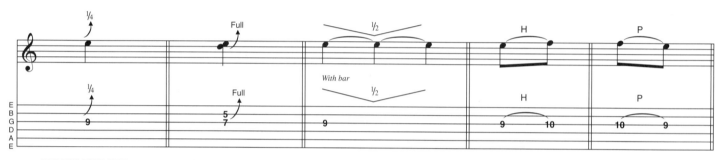

QUARTER-TONE BEND: Bend the note slightly sharp.

UNISON BEND: Strike both notes, then bend the lower note up to the pitch of the higher one.

TREMOLO BAR BENDS: Strike the note, and push the bar down and up by the amounts indicated.

HAMMER-ON: Strike the first note, then sound the second by fretting it without picking.

PULL-OFF: Strike the higher note, then pull the finger off while keeping the lower one fretted.

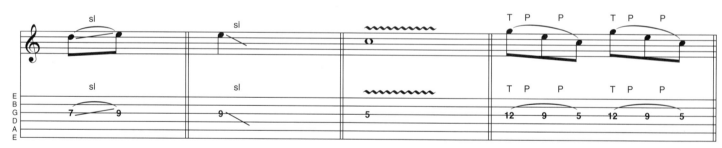

SLIDE: Slide the finger from the first note to the second. Only the first note is struck.

SLIDE: Slide to the fret from a few frets below or above.

VIBRATO: The string is vibrated by rapidly bending and releasing a note with the fretboard hand or tremolo bar.

TAPPING: Hammer on to the note marked with a T using the picking hand, then pull off to the next note, following the hammer-ons or pull-offs in the normal way.

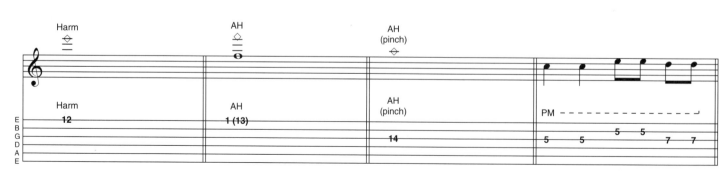

NATURAL HARMONIC: Lightly touch the string directly over the fret shown, then strike the note to create a "chiming" effect.

ARTIFICIAL HARMONIC: Fret the note, then use the picking hand finger to touch the string at the position shown in brackets and pluck with another finger.

ARTIFICIAL HARMONIC: The harmonic is produced by using the edge of the picking hand thumb to "pinch" the string whilst picking firmly with the plectrum.

PALM MUTES: Rest the palm of the picking hand on the strings near the bridge to produce a muted effect. Palm mutes can apply to a single note or a number of notes (shown with a dashed line).

Livin' On A Prayer

Words and Music by JON BON JOVI,
RICHIE SAMBORA and DESMOND CHILD

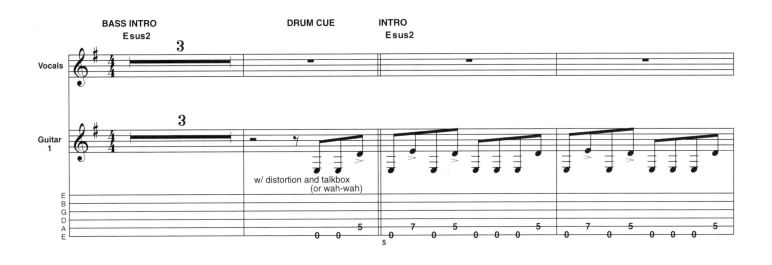

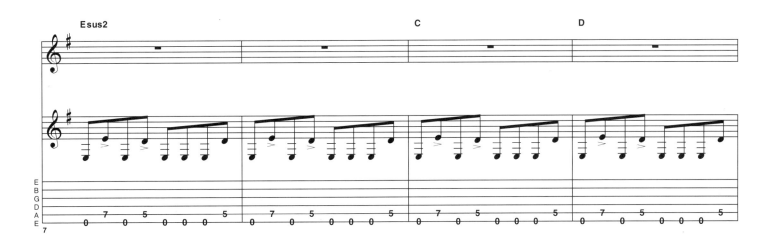

© Copyright 1986 Bon Jovi Publishing/EMI April Music Incorporated/Desmobile Music Company
Incorporated/PolyGram Music Publishing Incorporated, USA. Polygram Music Publishing Ltd, 47 British Grove,
London W4 (66.66%)/EMI Songs Limited, 127 Charing Cross Road, London WC2 (33.33%).
All Rights Reserved. International Copyright Secured.

not so long a-go

Tom-my used to work on the docks._____ Un-ion's been on strike, he's down on his luck, it's

tough,_____ so_____ tough._____

w/ talkbox

Gi-na works the di-ner all day,_____ work-ing for her man she brings home her pay, for love,—

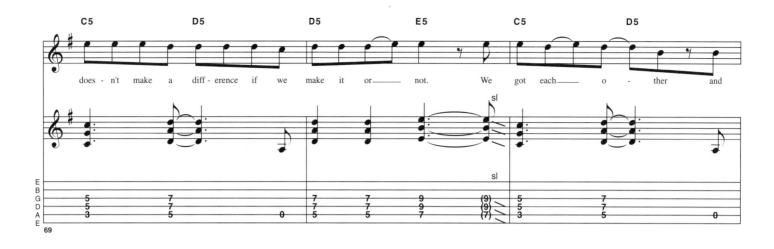

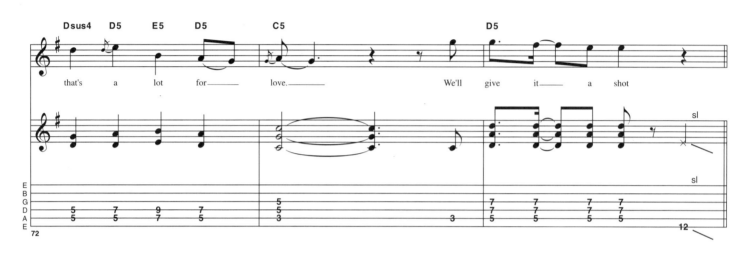

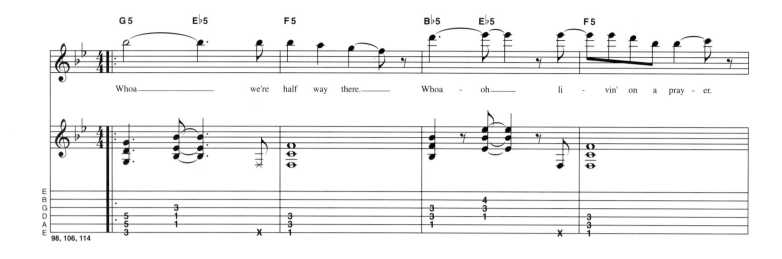

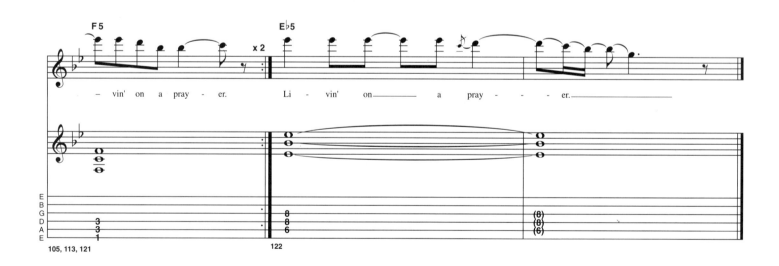

Wanted Dead Or Alive

Words and Music by JON BON JOVI
and RICHIE SAMBORA

© Copyright 1987 Bon Jovi Publishing/PolyGram Music Publishing Incorporated, USA.
Polygram Music Publishing Ltd, 47 British Grove, London W4.
All Rights Reserved. International Copyright Secured.

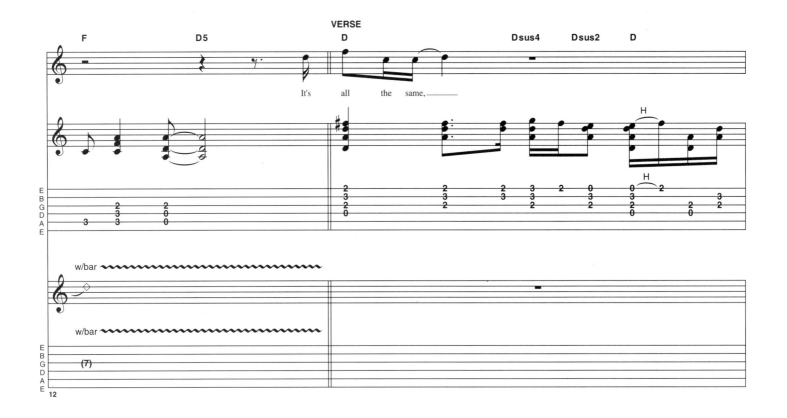

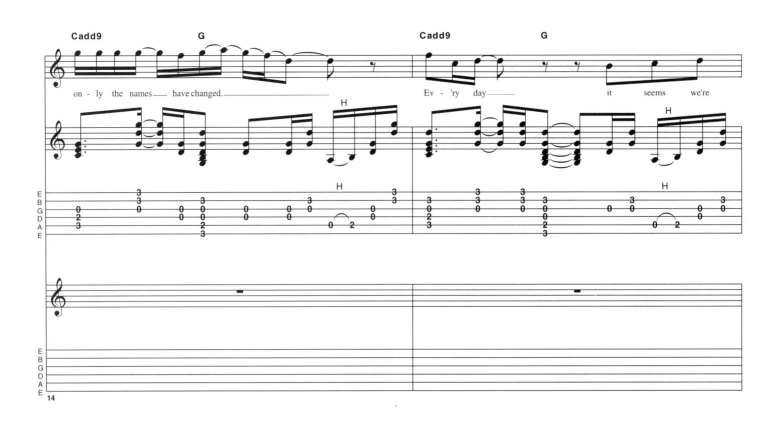

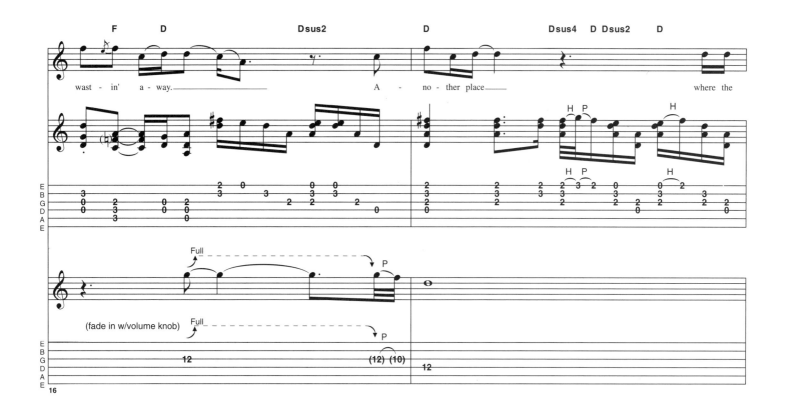

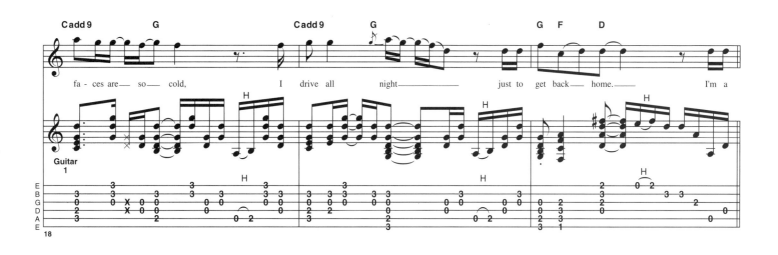

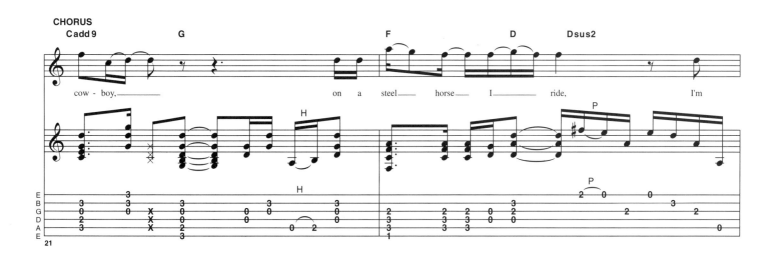

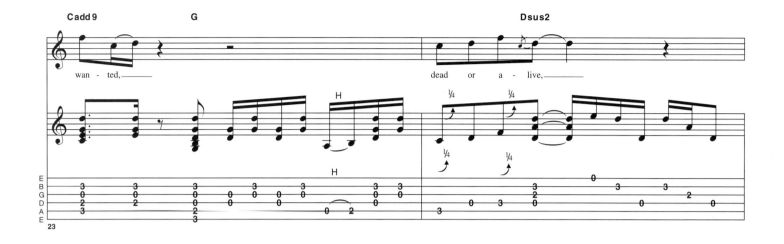

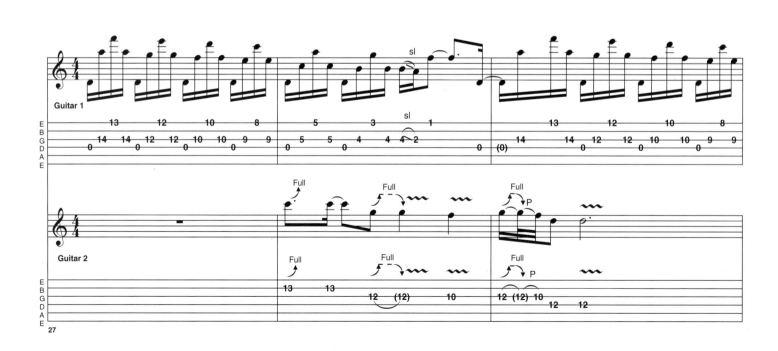

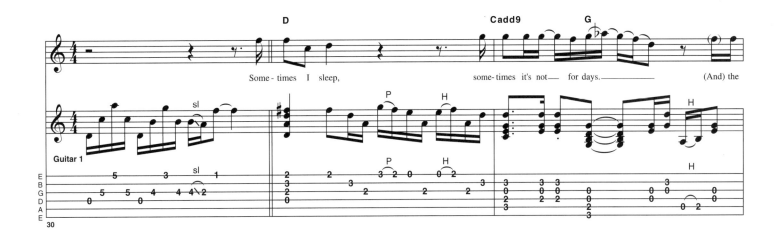

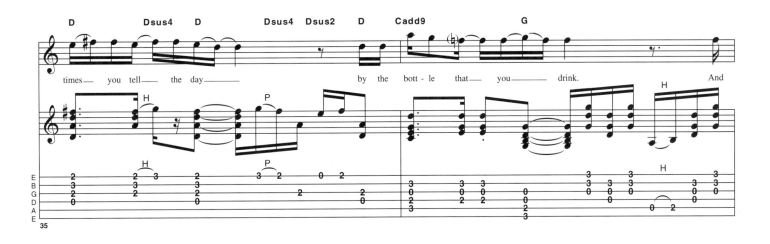

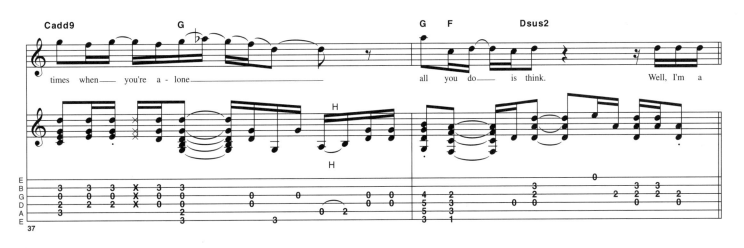

CHORUS

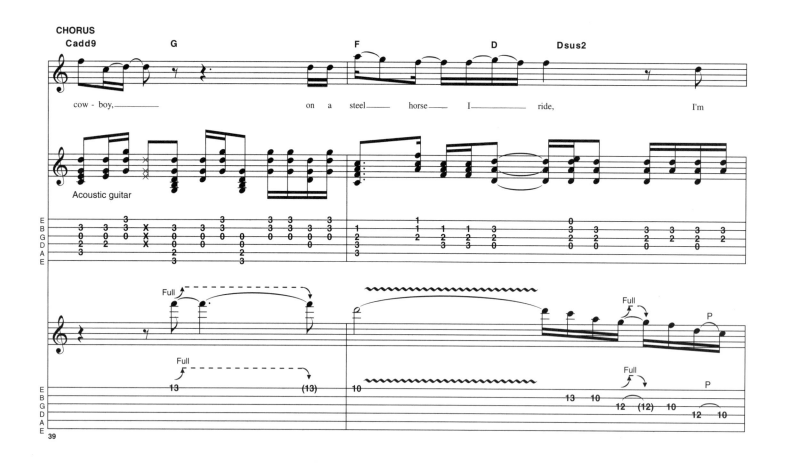

cow - boy,_____ on a steel_____ horse_____ I_____ ride,_____ I'm

Acoustic guitar

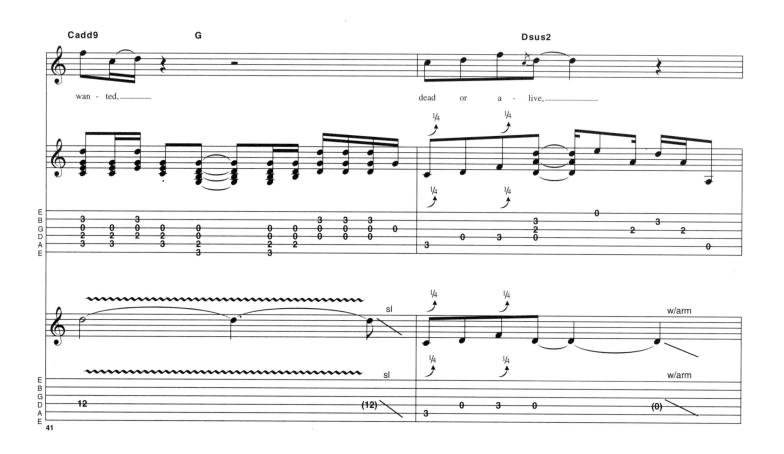

wan - ted,_____ dead or a - live,_____

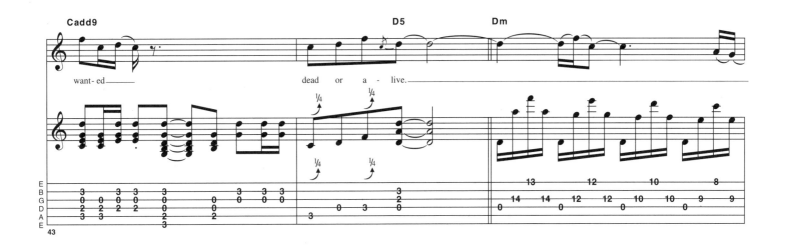

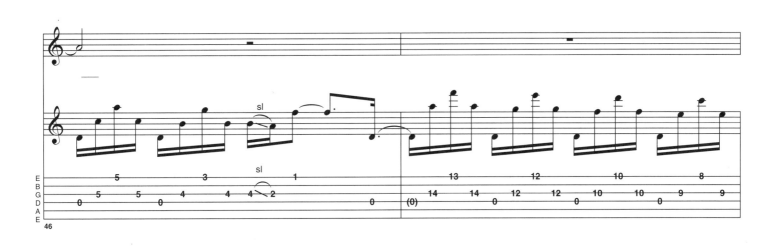

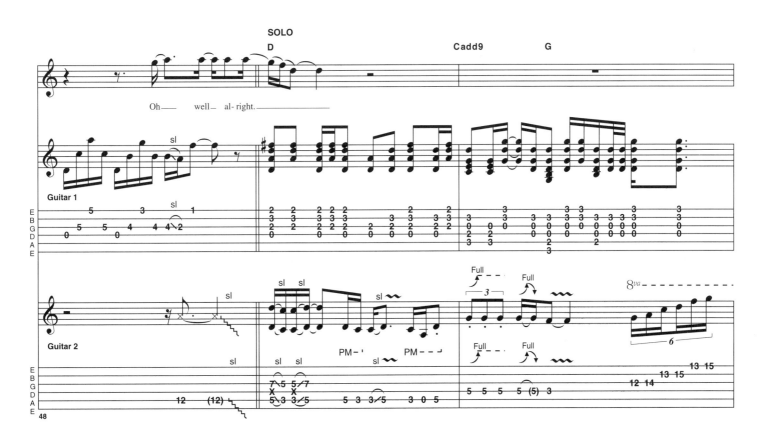

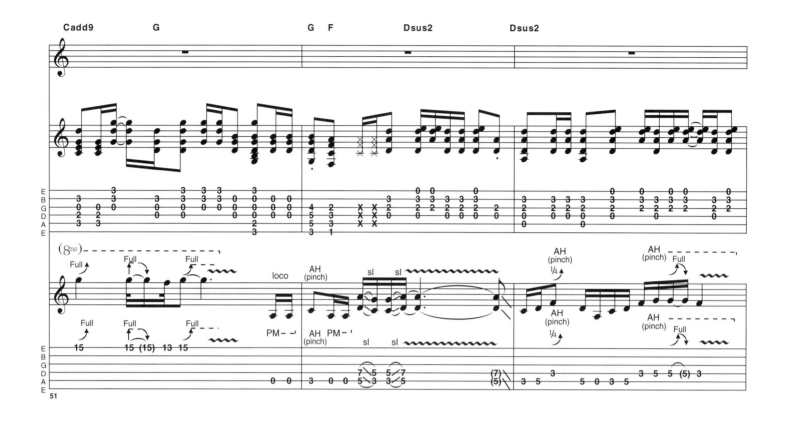

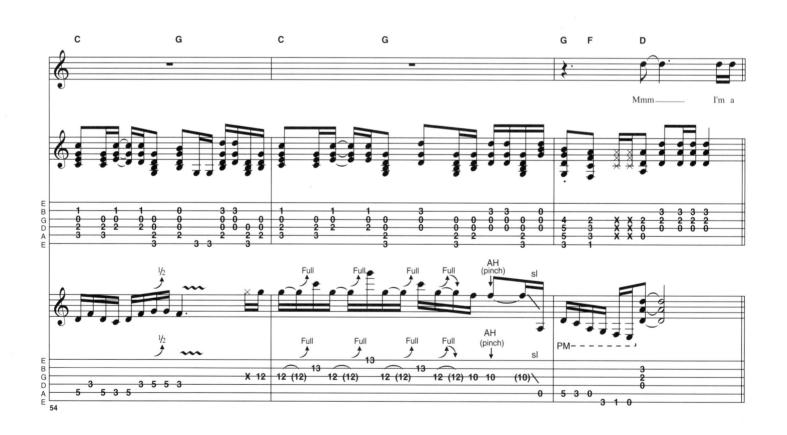

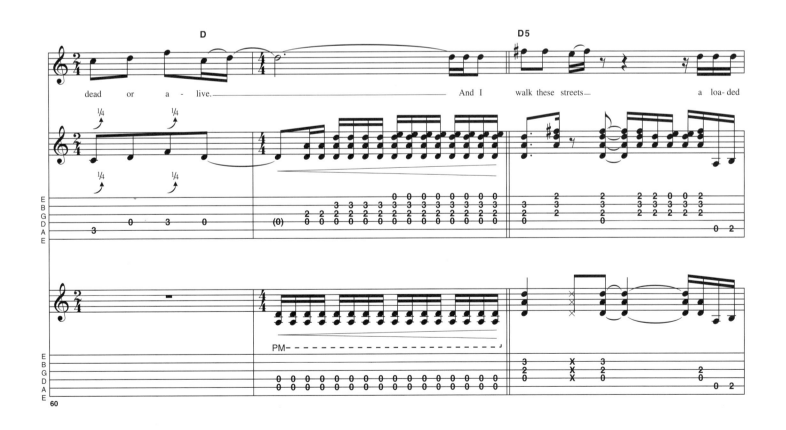

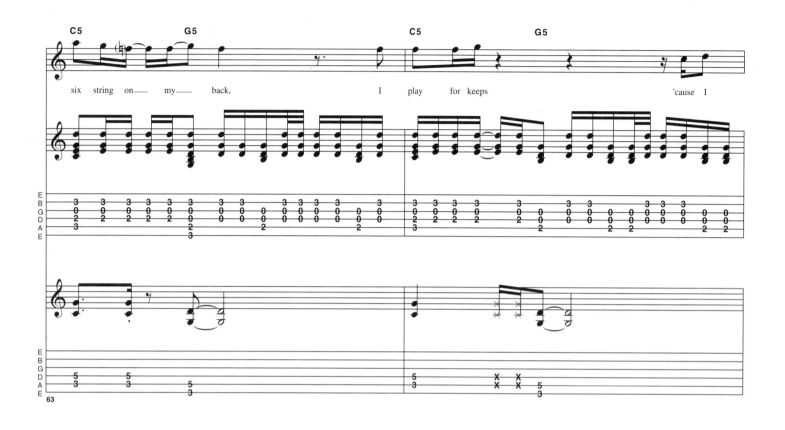

six string on— my— back,   I   play   for   keeps   'cause I

might   not   make— it   back.————   I've been   ev - 'ry where,———   still I'm

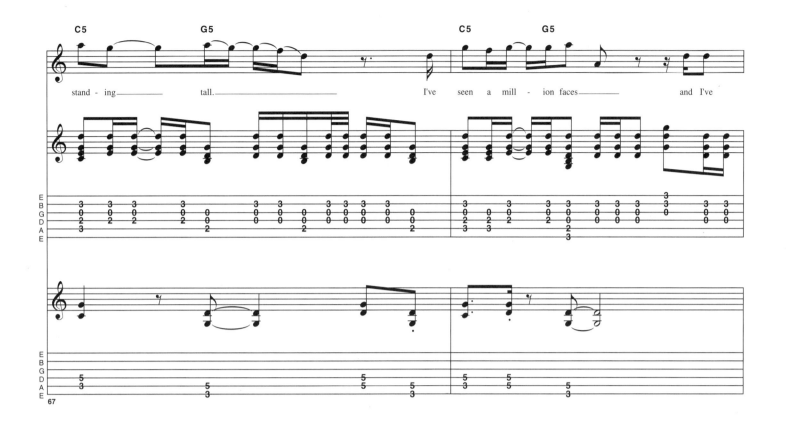

stand - ing———— tall.———————— I've seen a mill - ion faces———— and I've

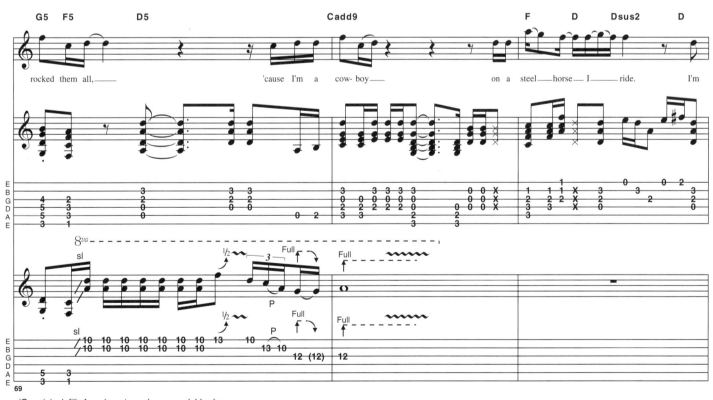

rocked them all,———— 'cause I'm a cow- boy———— on a steel——horse— I— ride. I'm

(On original, fills from here to end are overdubbed on
separate track and gtr 2 continues with power chords)

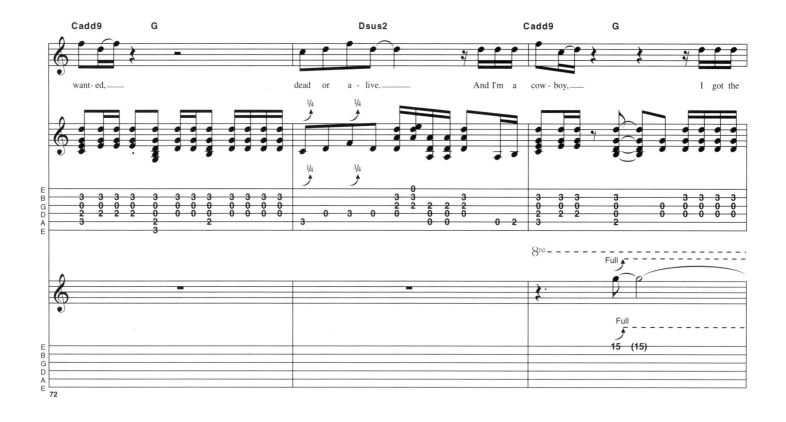

want- ed,_____ dead or a - live._____ And I'm a cow - boy,_____ I got the

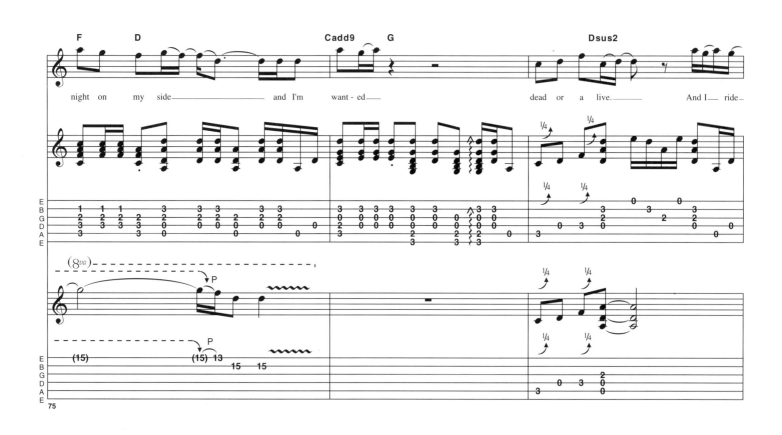

night on my side_____ and I'm want - ed dead or a live._____ And I__ ride__

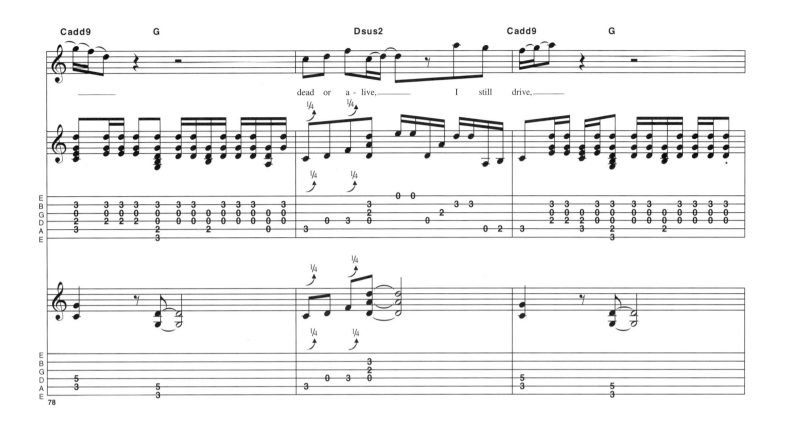

dead or a - live,_____ I still drive,_____

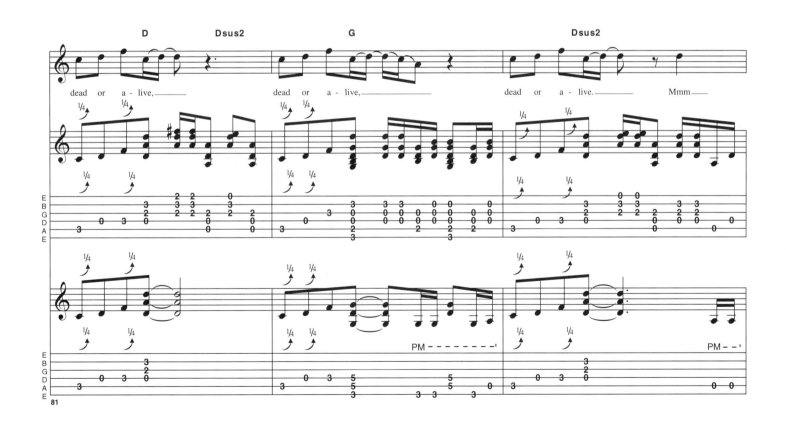

dead or a - live,_____ dead or a - live,_____ dead or a - live._____ Mmm_____

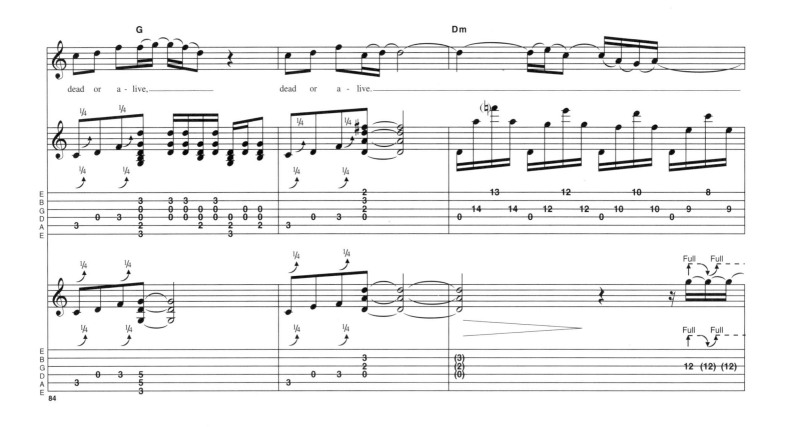

dead or a - live,_____ dead or a - live._____

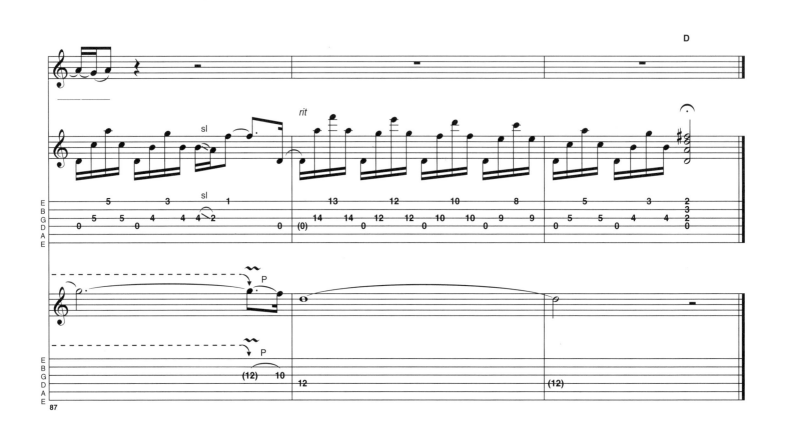

You Give Love A Bad Name

Words and Music by JON BON JOVI,
RICHIE SAMBORA and DESMOND CHILD

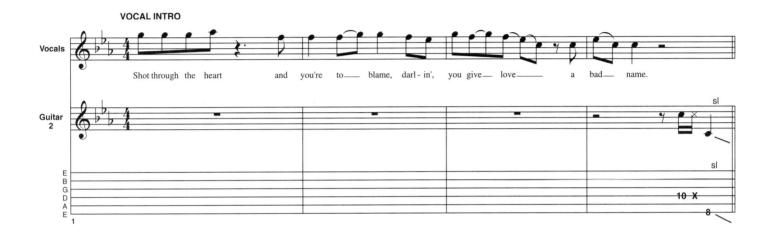

© Copyright 1986 Bon Jovi Publishing/EMI April Music Incorporated/Desmobile Music Company
Incorporated/PolyGram Music Publishing Incorporated, USA. Polygram Music Publishing Ltd, 47 British Grove,
London W4 (66.66%)/EMI Songs Limited, 127 Charing Cross Road, London WC2 (33.33%).
All Rights Reserved. International Copyright Secured.

an- gel's smile —— is what you sell, you prom- ised me hea- ven and put me through hell.
Paint your smile —— on your lips, blood red nails on your fin - ger tips.— A

Chains of — love —— got a hold on me, when pass - ion's a pris - on you can't break — free.
school- boy's— dream —— you act so shy, your ver - y first kiss was your first kiss good- bye.

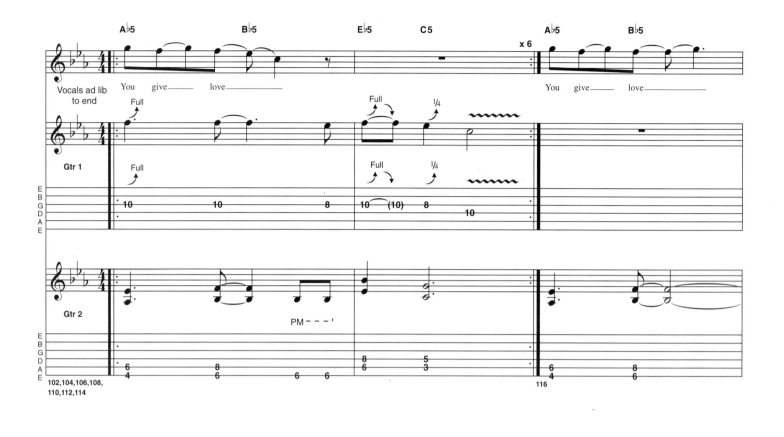

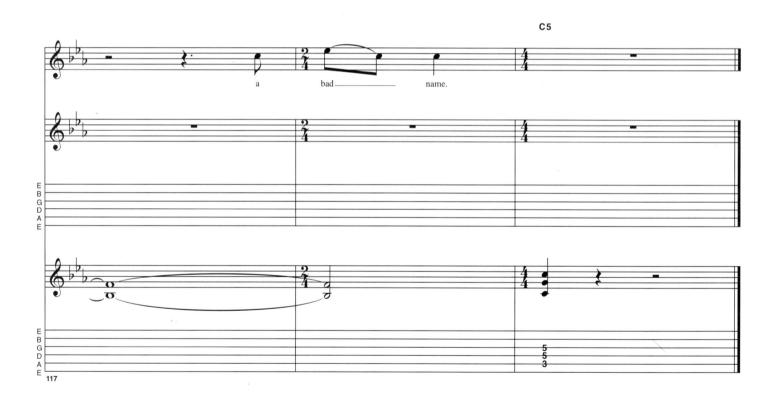

Dry County

Words and Music by JON BON JOVI

© Copyright 1992 PolyGram International Publishing Incorporated/Bon Jovi Publishing, USA.
PolyGram Music Publishing Limited, 47 British Grove, London W4.
All Rights Reserved. International Copyright Secured.

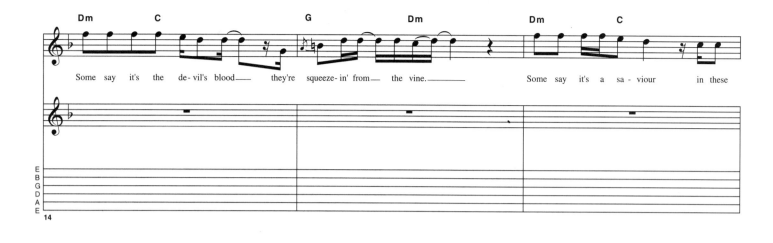

Some say it's the de- vil's blood—— they're squeeze- in' from—— the vine.—— Some say it's a sa - viour in these

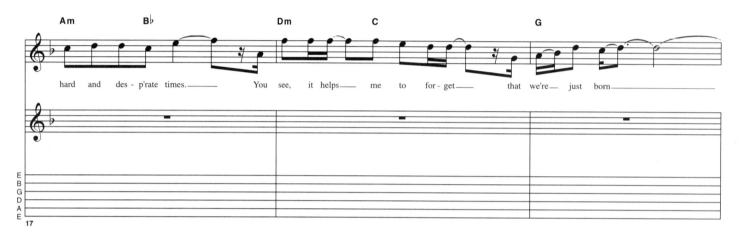

hard and des - p'rate times.—— You see, it helps—— me to for - get—— that we're—— just born——

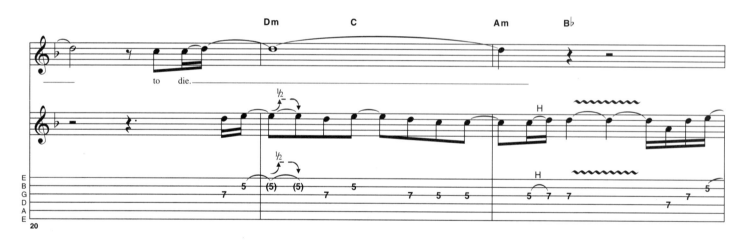

to die.——

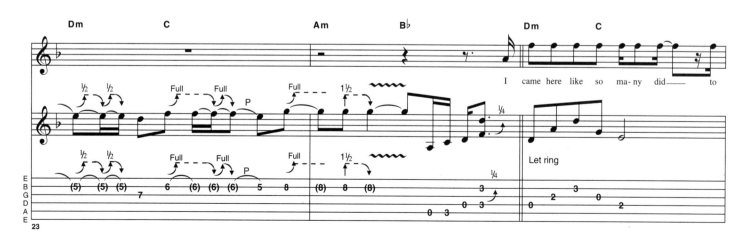

I came here like so ma- ny did—— to

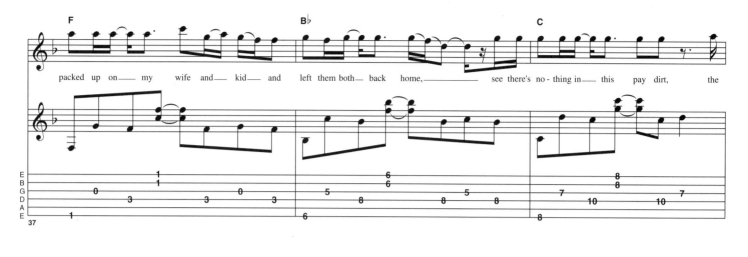

packed up on— my wife and— kid— and left them both— back home,———— see there's no - thing in— this pay dirt, the

ghosts are all— I know. Now the oil's— gone———— and the mo - ney's gone,———— all the

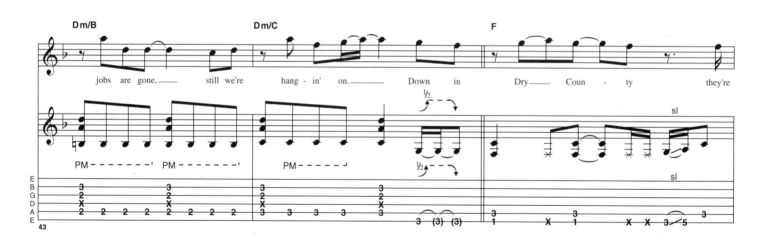

jobs are gone,———— still we're hang - in' on.———— Down in Dry— Coun - ty they're

swim - min' in— the sand,———— pray - in' for———— some ho - ly wa - ter to wash these sins from off our hands.— In

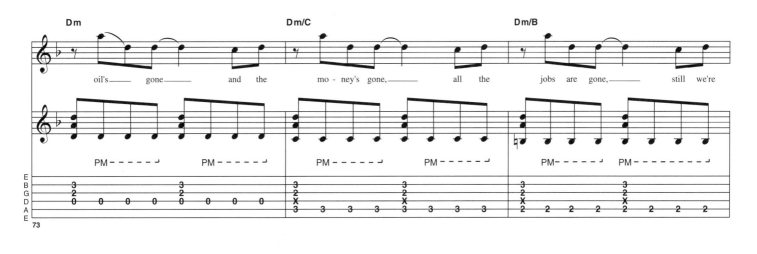

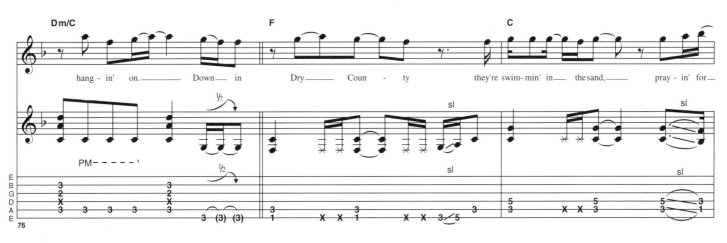

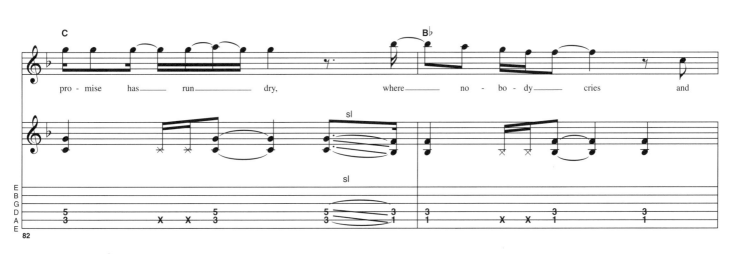

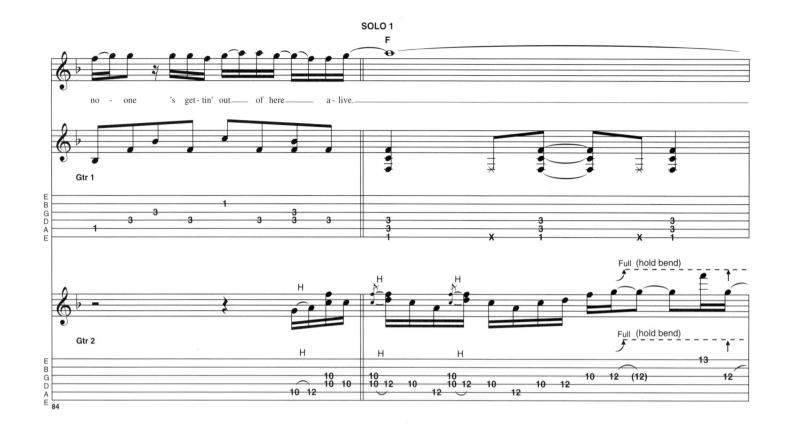

no - one 's get-tin' out___ of here___ a - live.___

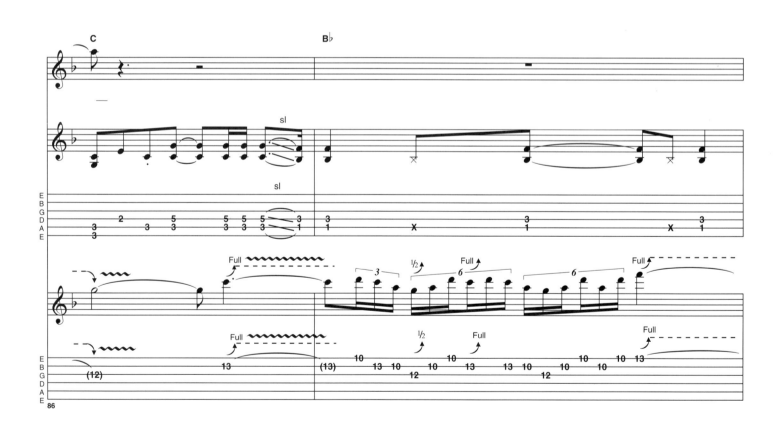

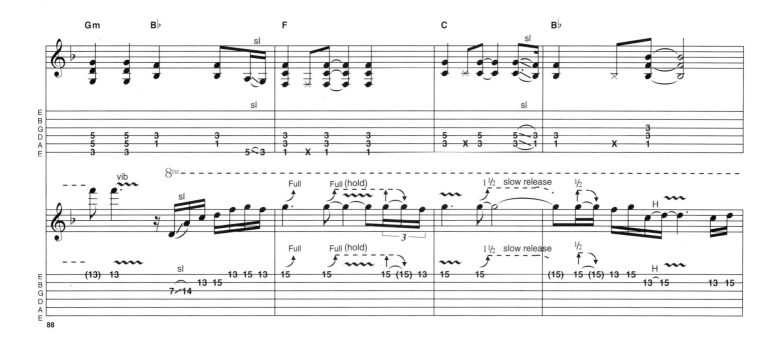

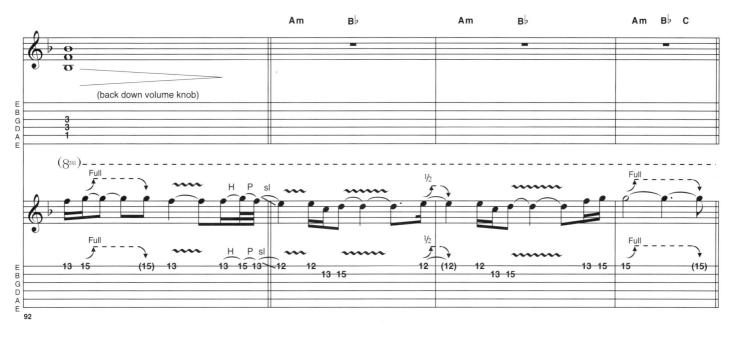

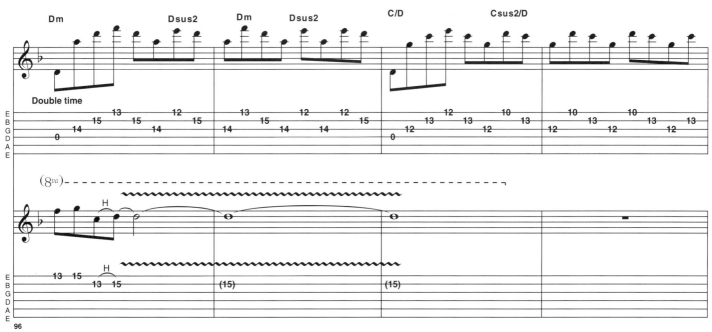

48

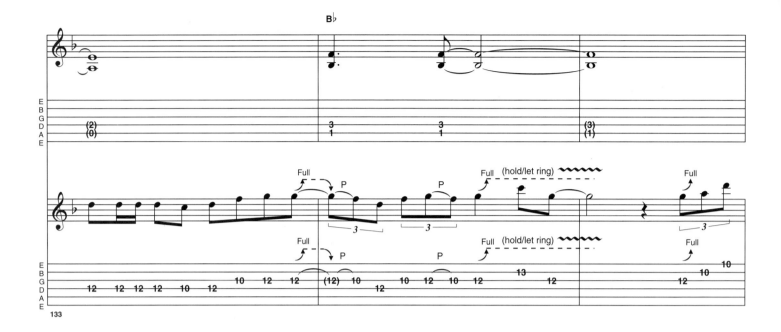

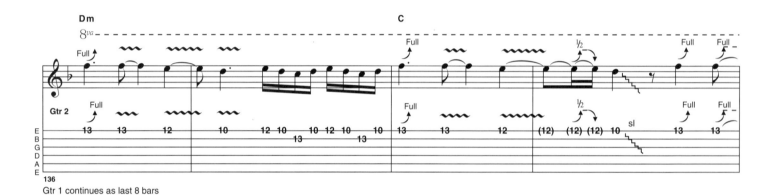

Gtr 1 continues as last 8 bars

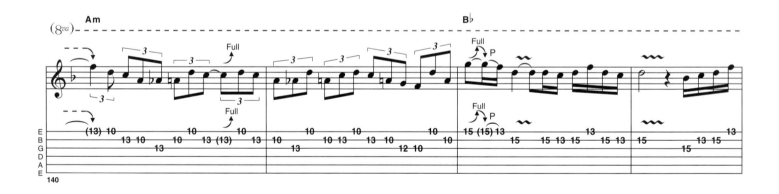

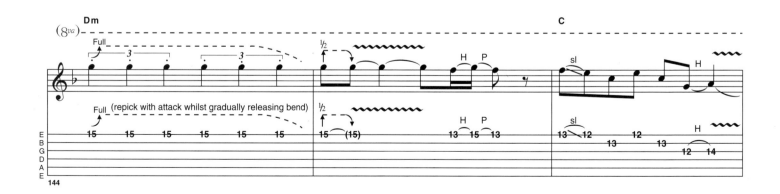

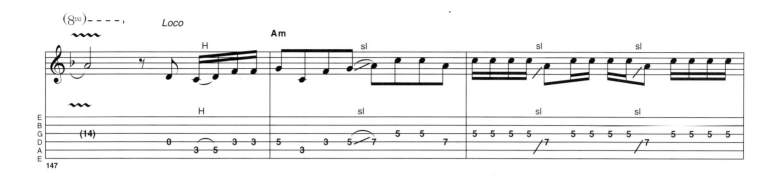

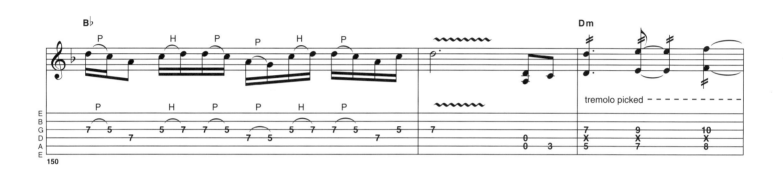

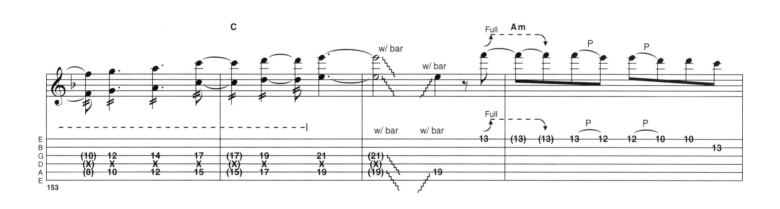

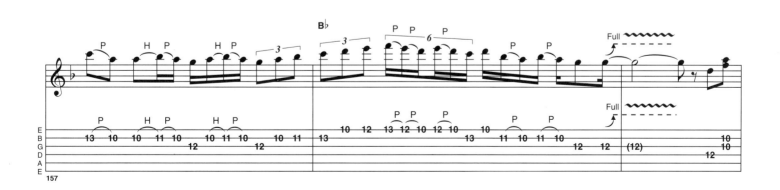

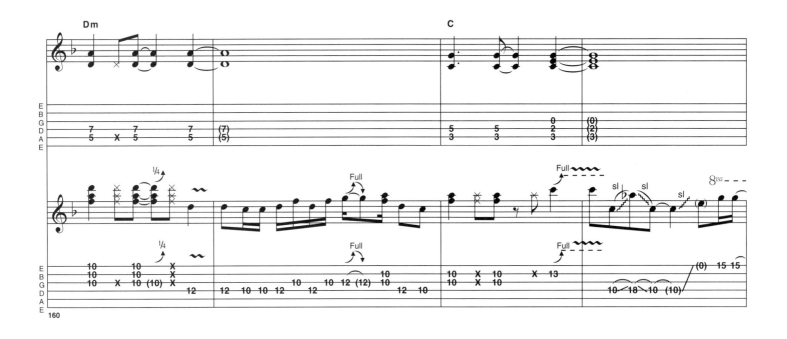

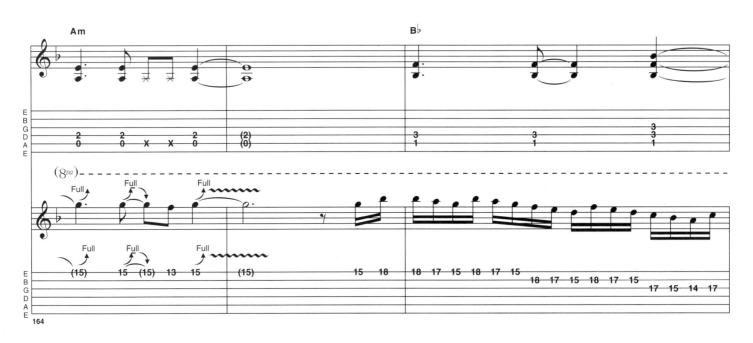

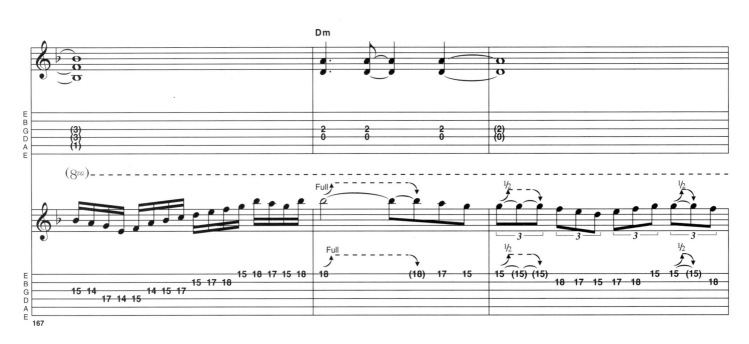

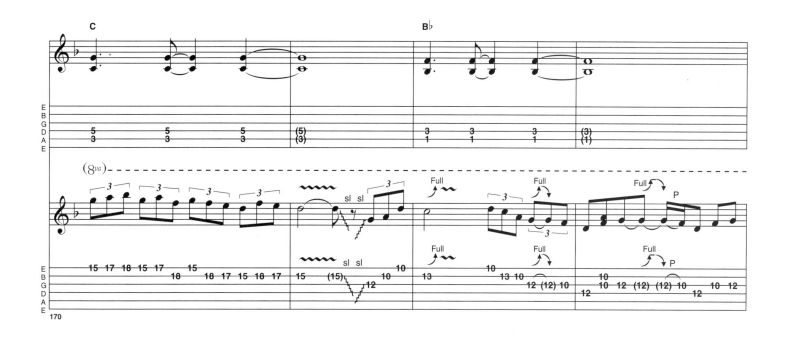

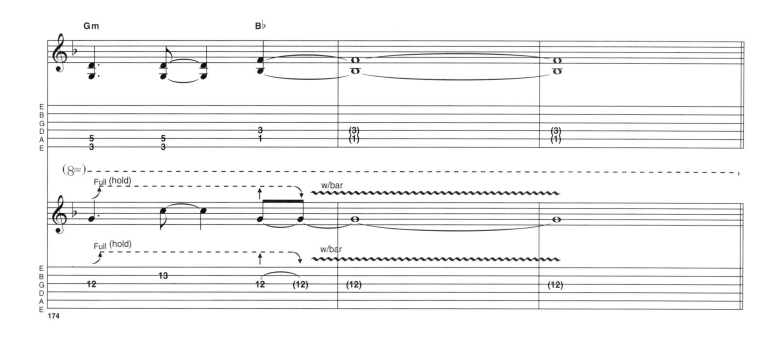

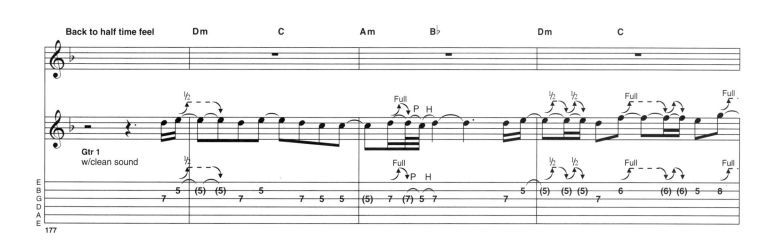

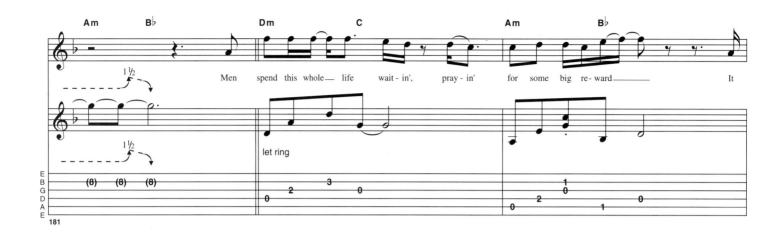

Men spend this whole—— life wait-in', pray-in' for some big re-ward—— It

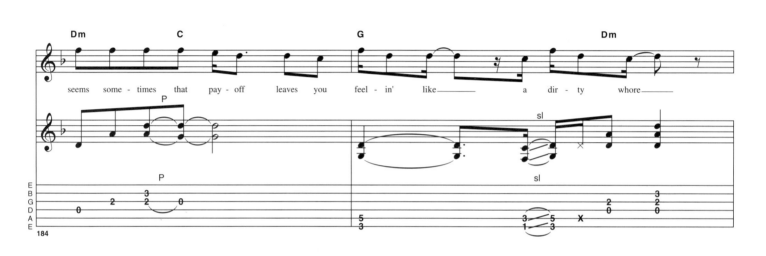

seems some - times that pay-off leaves you feel - in' like—— a dir - ty whore——

(If) I could choose the way I die—— make it by the gun or knife—— 'cause the

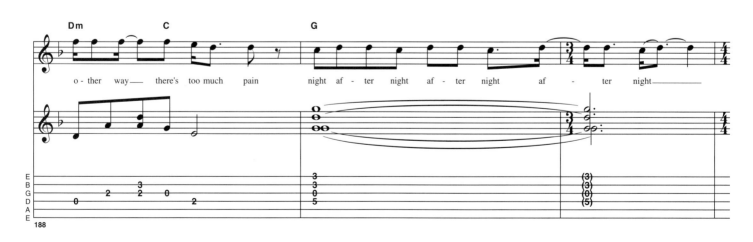

o - ther way—— there's too much pain night af - ter night af - ter night af - ter night——

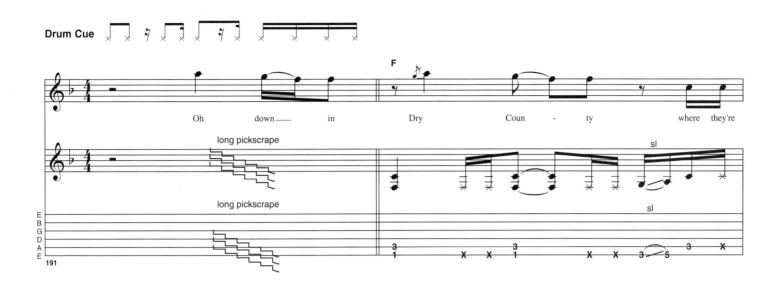

Oh down— in Dry Coun-ty where they're

swim out in— the sand— pray-in' for— some hol-y wa-ter to wash these sins from off our hands— in

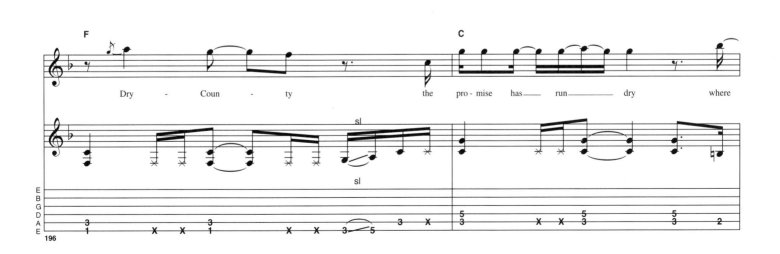

Dry-Coun-ty the pro-mise has— run— dry where

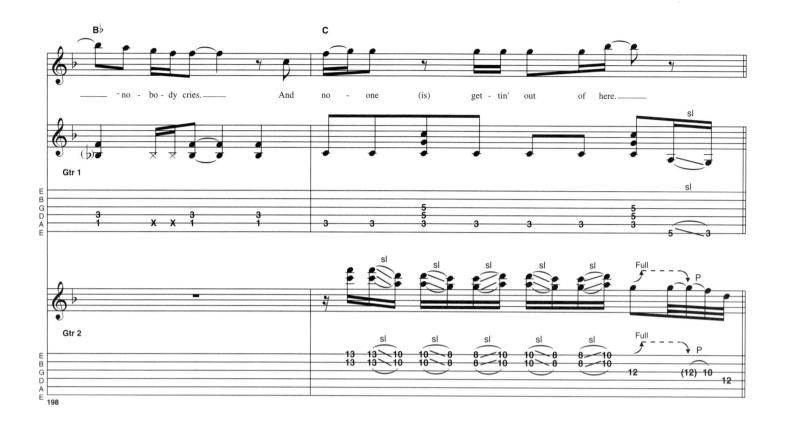

- no - bo - dy cries.____ And no - one (is) get - tin' out of here.____

(Vocal improvisation over next Chorus)

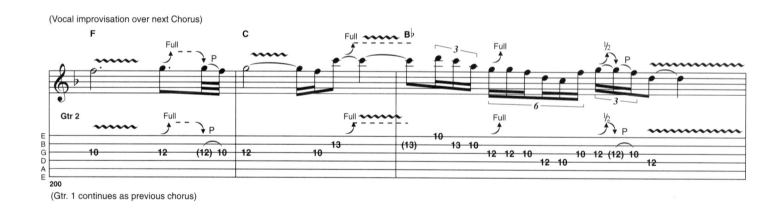

(Gtr. 1 continues as previous chorus)

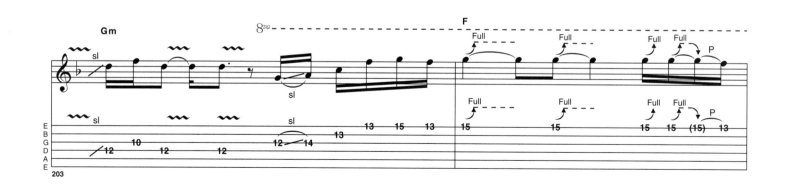

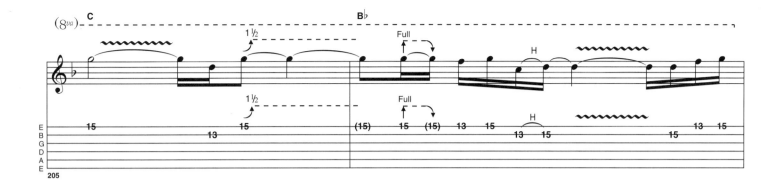

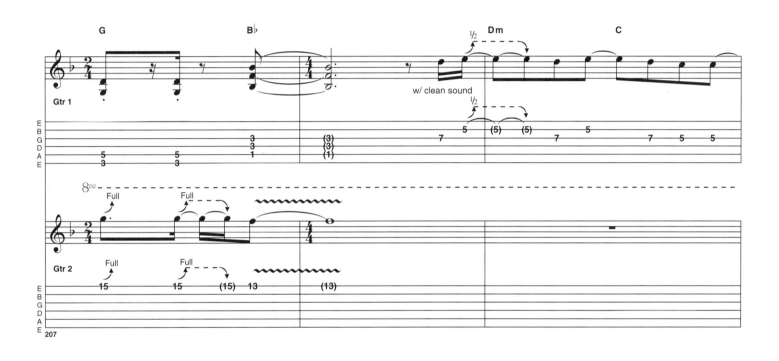

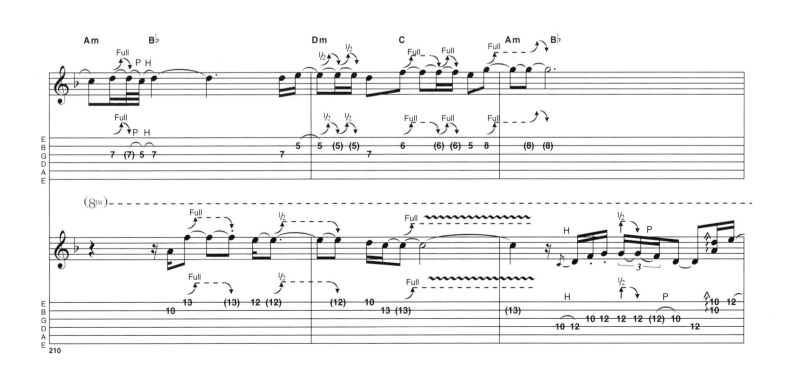

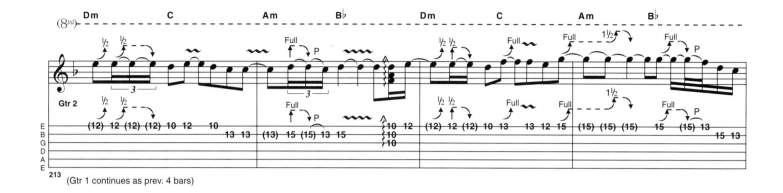

213 (Gtr 1 continues as prev. 4 bars)

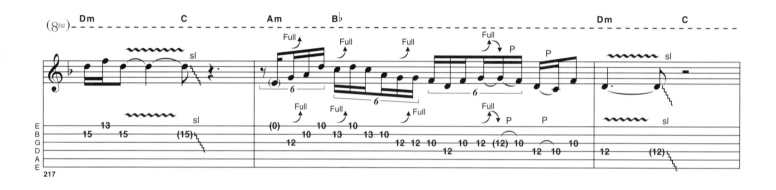

217

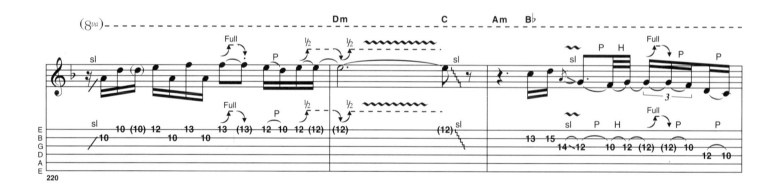

220

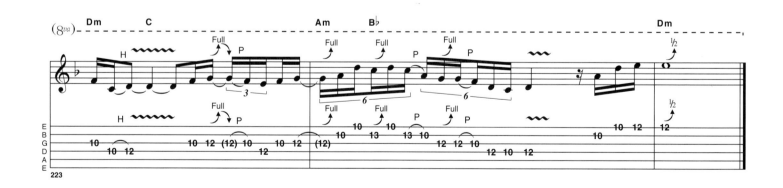

223

In These Arms

Words and Music by JON BON JOVI,
RICHIE SAMBORA and DAVID BRYAN

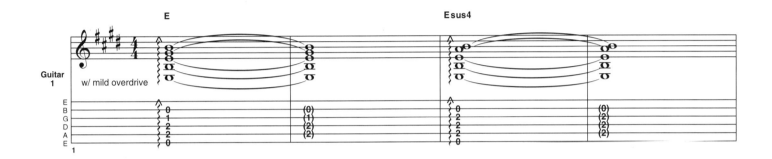

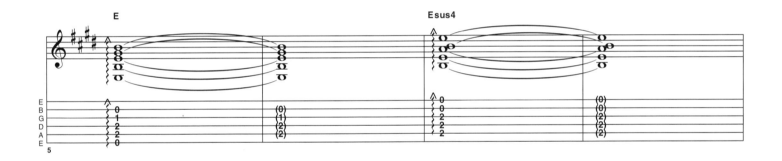

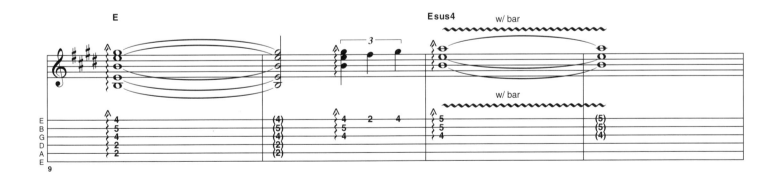

© Copyright 1992 PolyGram International Music Publishing Incorporated/Bon Jovi Publishing/Aggressive
Music & David Bryan Music USA. Polygram Music Publishing Ltd, 47 British Grove,
London W4. All Rights Reserved. International Copyright Secured.

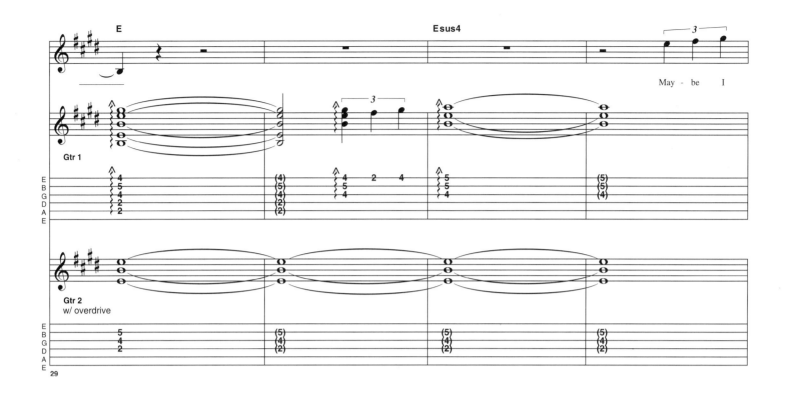

May - be I

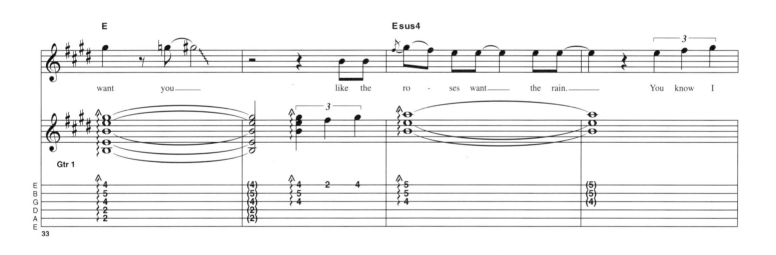

want you_____ like the ro - ses want_____ the rain._____ You know I

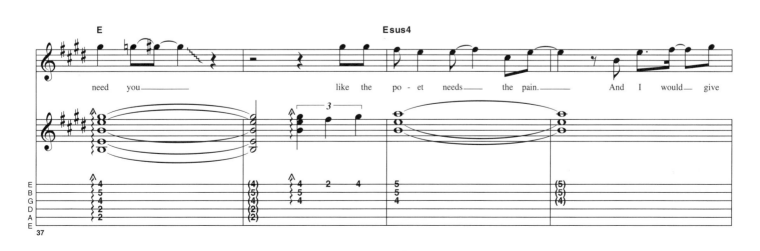

need you_____ like the po - et needs_____ the pain._____ And I would_____ give

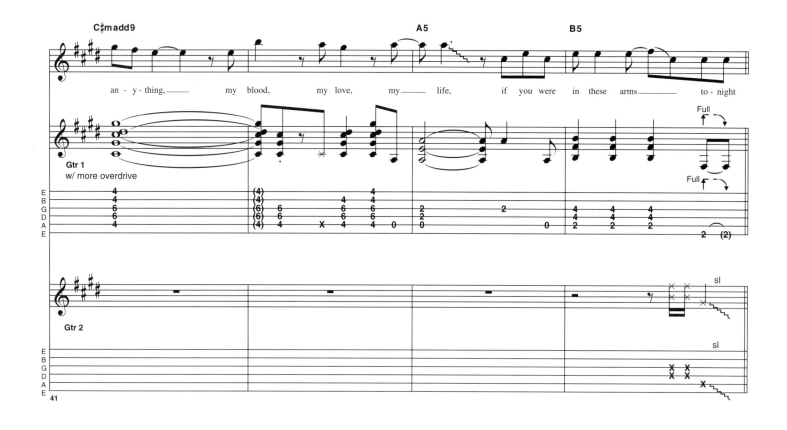

an-y-thing,___ my blood, my love, my___ life, if you were in these arms___ to-night

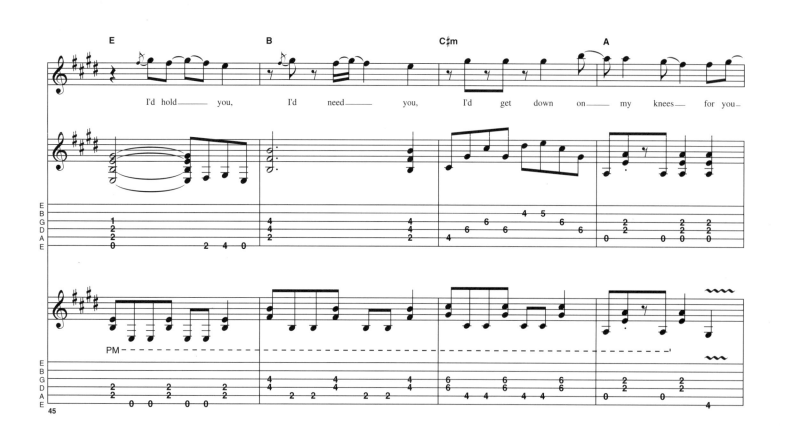

I'd hold___ you, I'd need___ you, I'd get down on___ my knees___ for you___

and make ev - 'ry thing — all - right. — If you were in these arms —

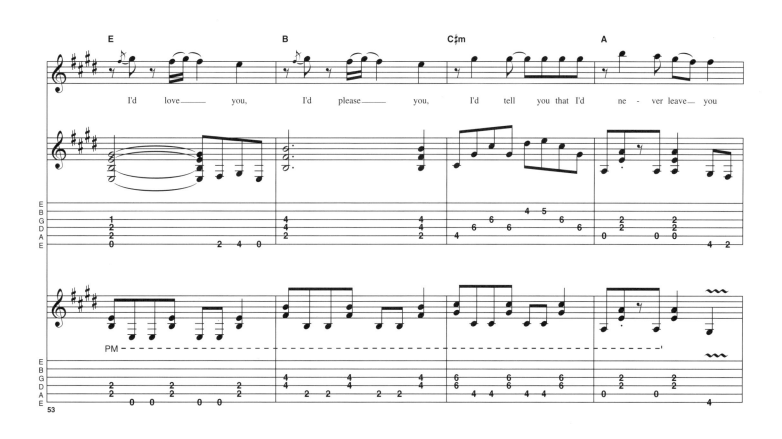

I'd love — you, I'd please — you, I'd tell you that I'd ne - ver leave— you

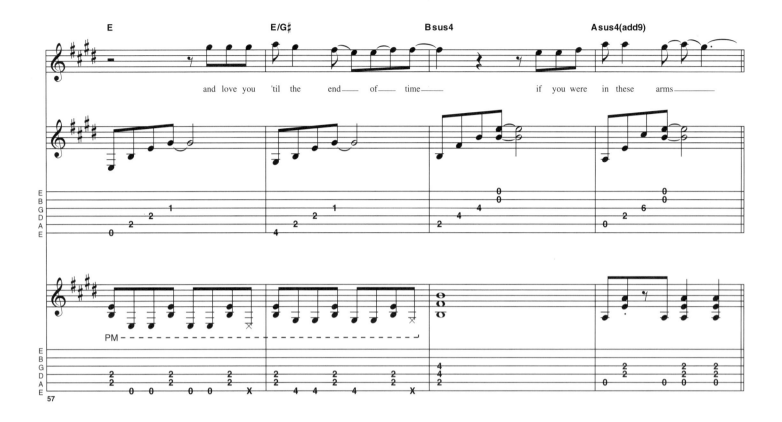

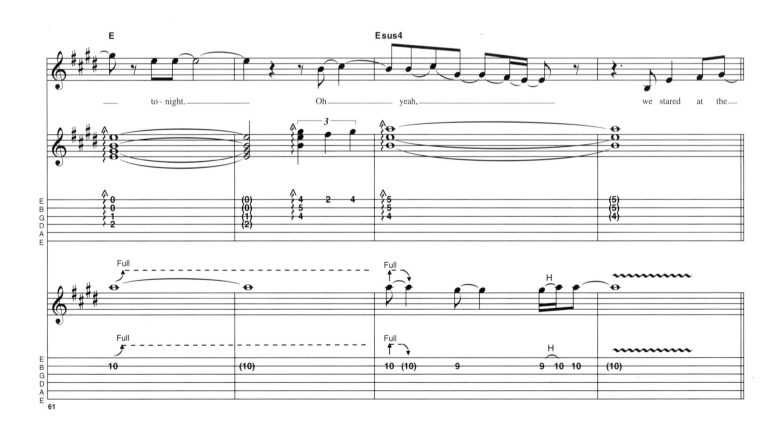

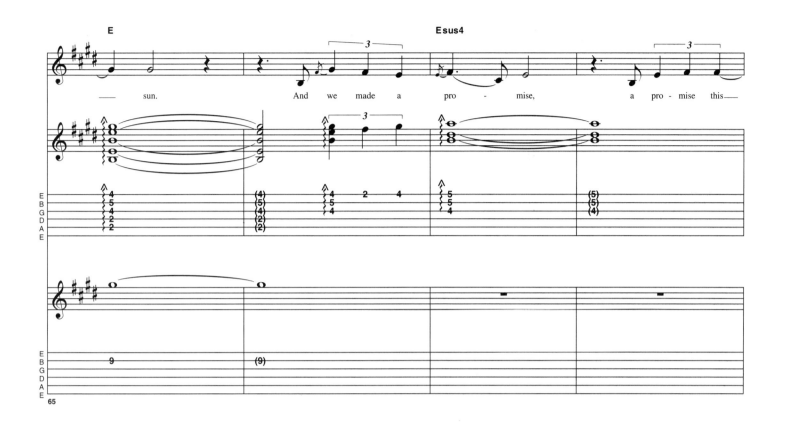

— sun.   And we made a pro - mise,   a pro - mise this —

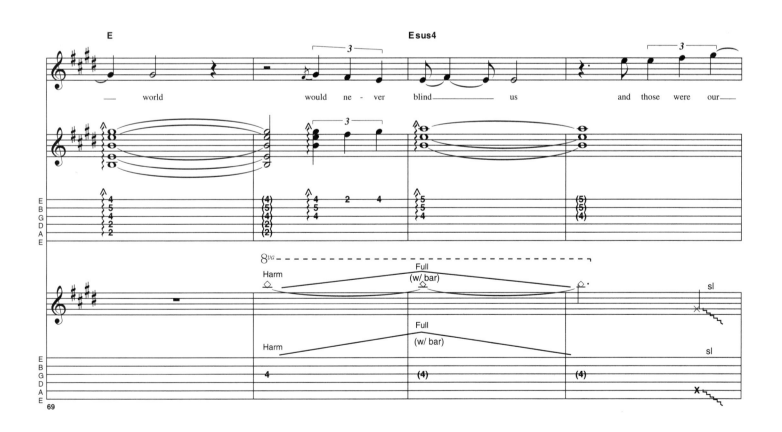

— world   would ne - ver blind ———— us   and those were our —

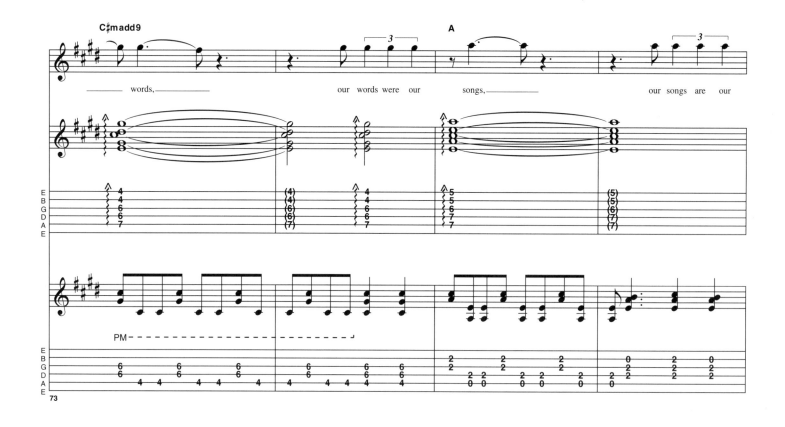

words, _____ our words were our songs, _____ our songs are our

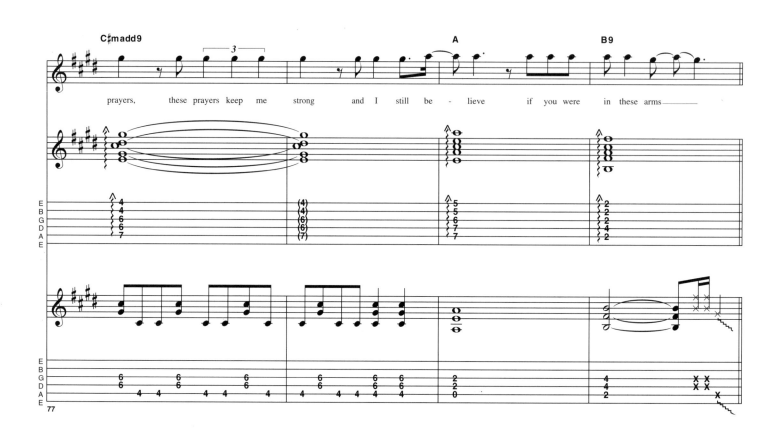

prayers, these prayers keep me strong and I still be - lieve if you were in these arms _____

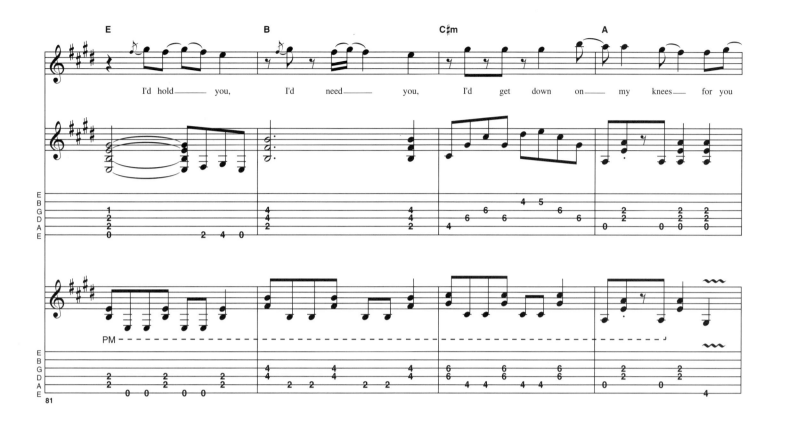

I'd hold———— you, I'd need———— you, I'd get down on—— my knees—— for you

———— and make ev-'ry thing—— all - right.———— If you were in these arms————

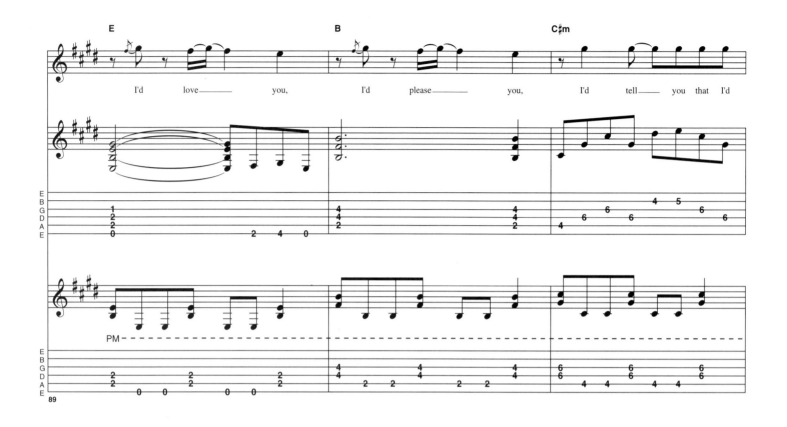

I'd love_____ you, I'd please_____ you, I'd tell_____ you that I'd

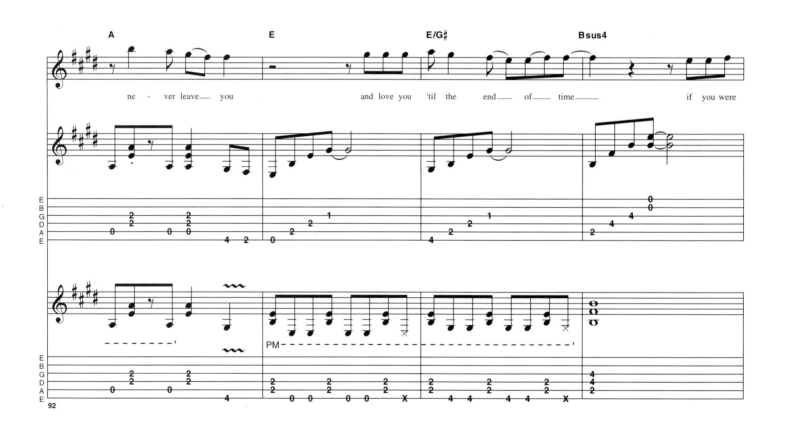

ne - ver leave___ you and love you 'til the end___ of___ time_____ if you were

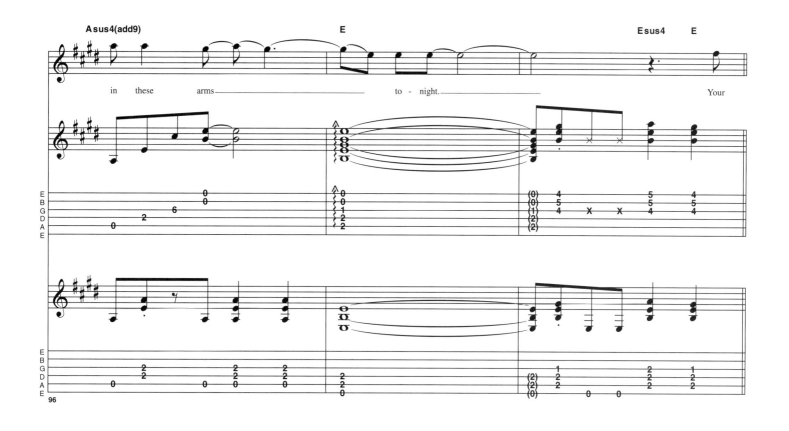

in these arms————————— to - night.————————— Your

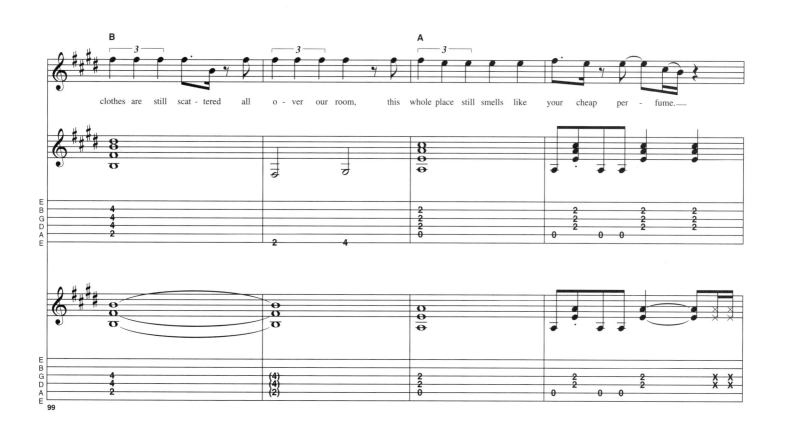

clothes are still scat - tered all o - ver our room, this whole place still smells like your cheap per - fume.——

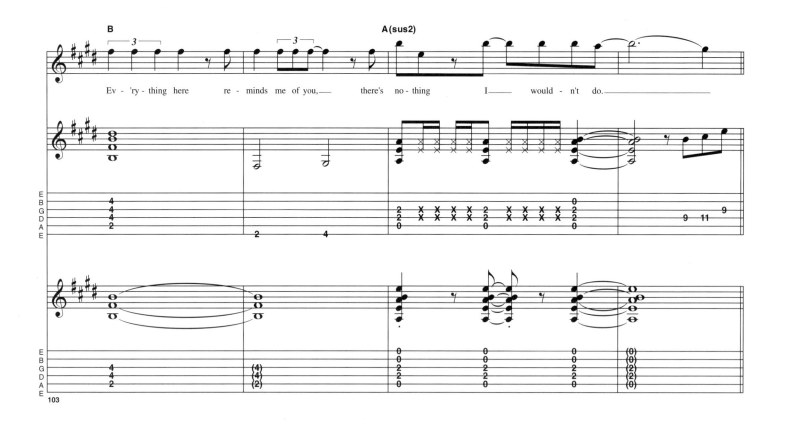

Ev - 'ry - thing here re - minds me of you,— there's no - thing I— would - n't do.—

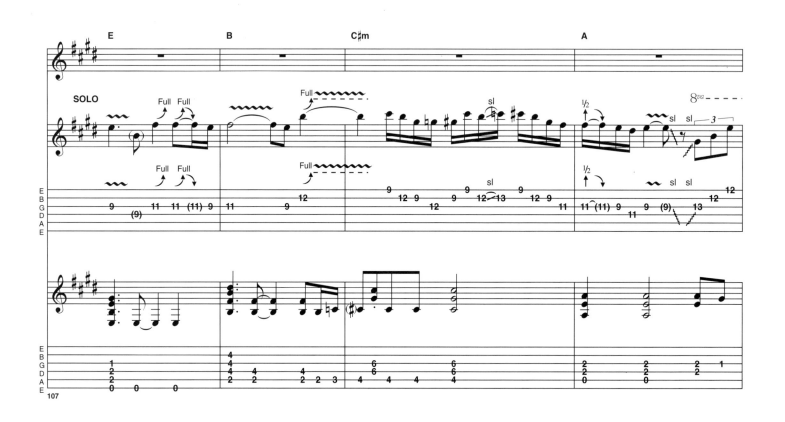

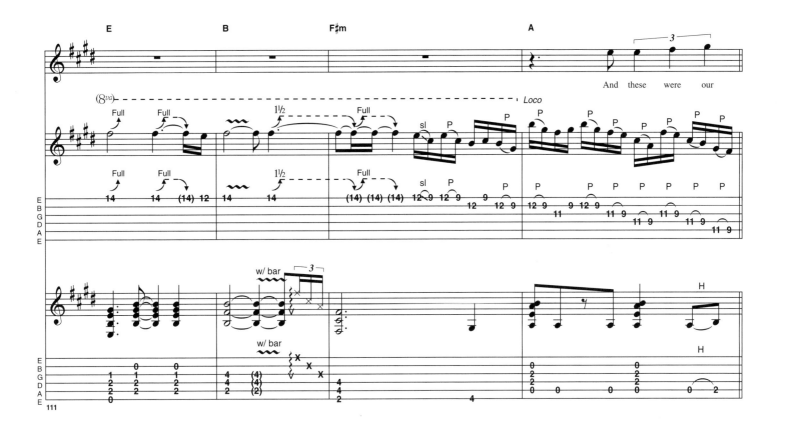

And these were our

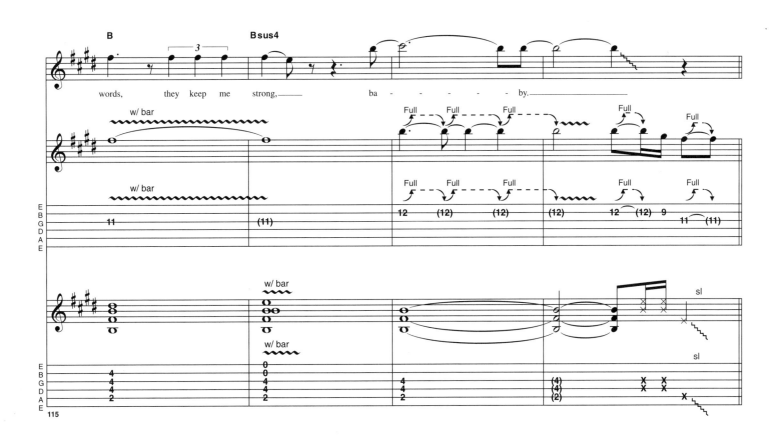

words, they keep me strong,_____ ba - - - - - by._____

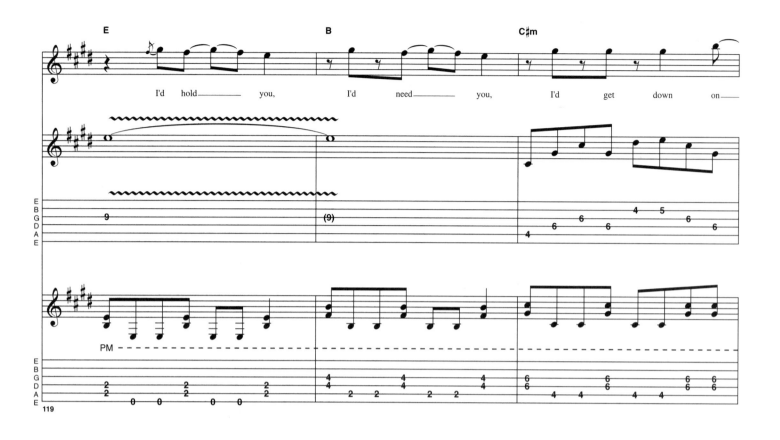

I'd hold_____ you, I'd need_____ you, I'd get down on_____

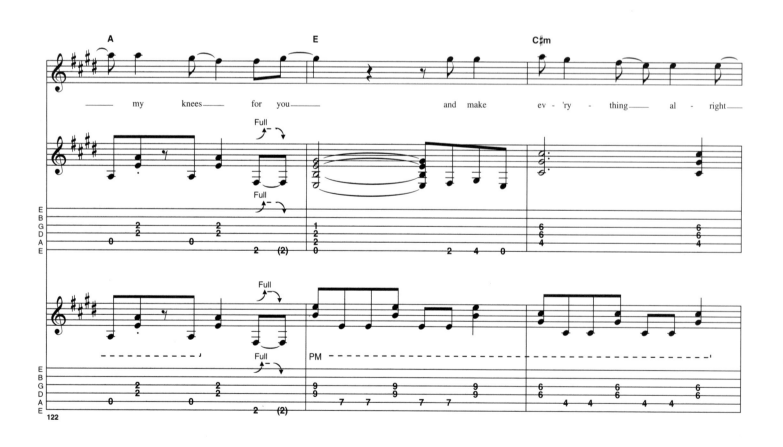

_____ my knees_____ for you_____ and make ev - 'ry - thing_____ al - right_____

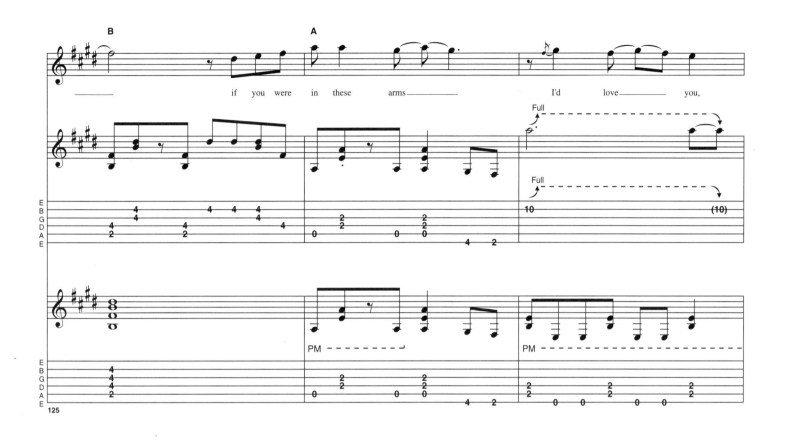

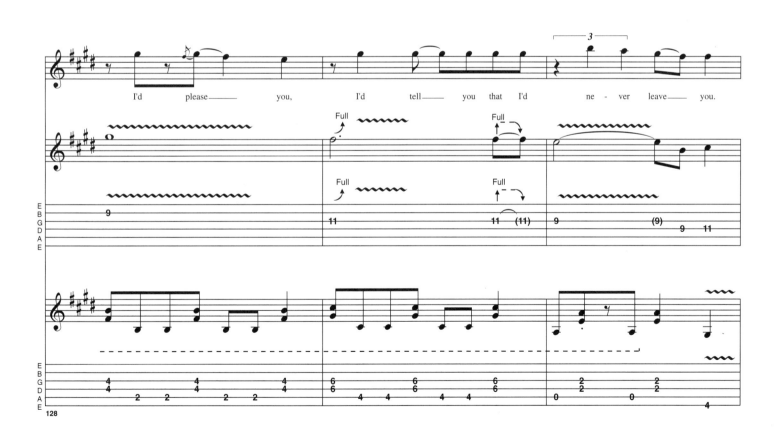

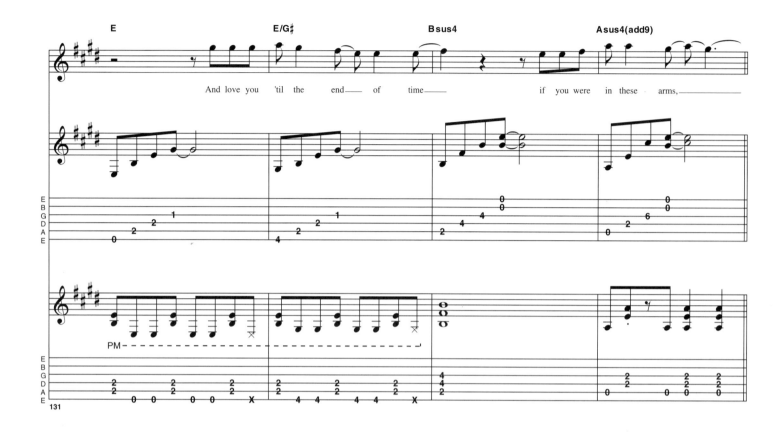

And love you 'til the end— of time—— if you were in these arms,——

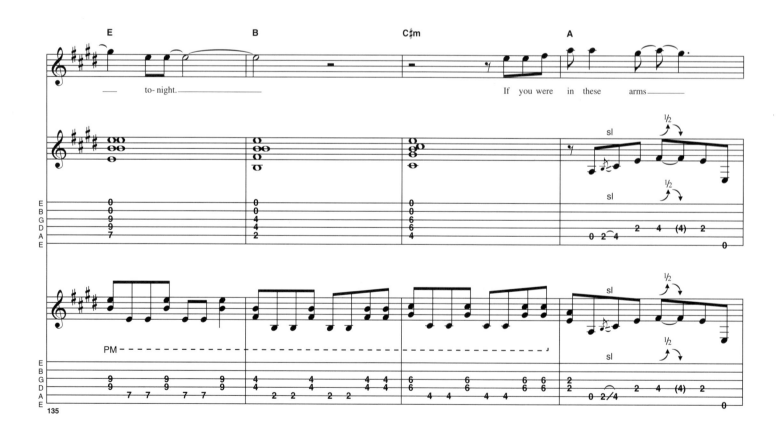

— to-night.———— If you were in these arms———

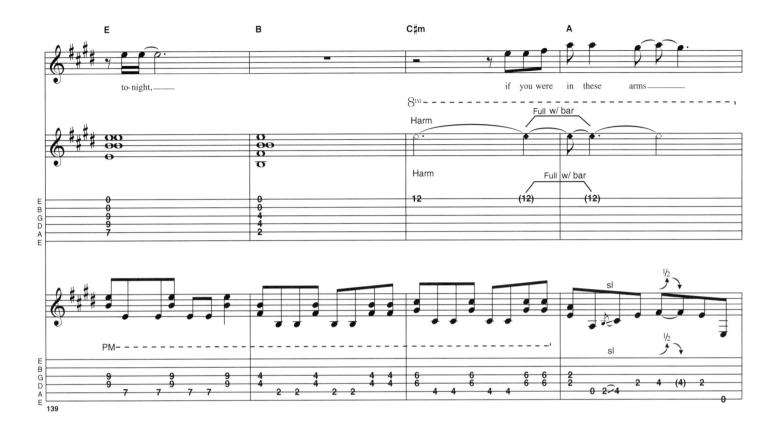

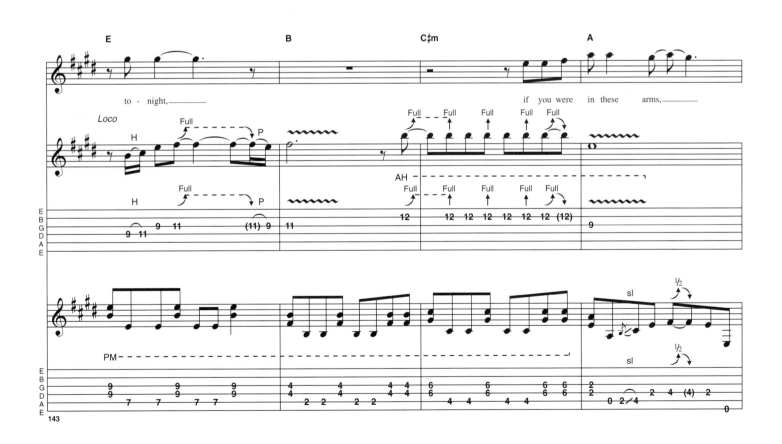

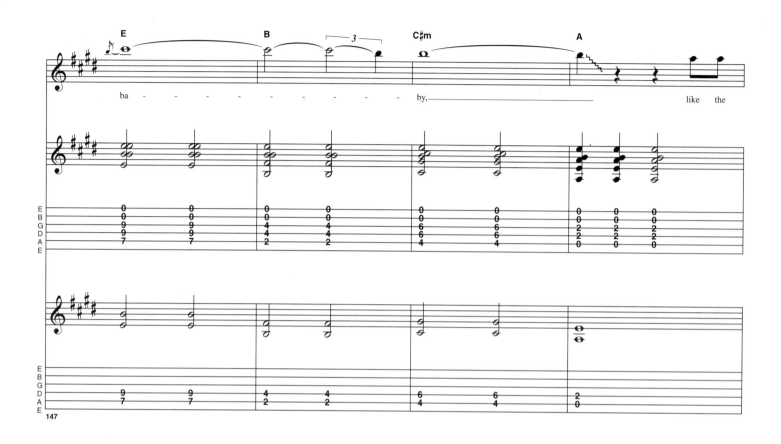

ba - - - - - - - by,_____ like the

ros - es need_____ the rain,_____ like the sea- sons need_____ to change,_____ like the

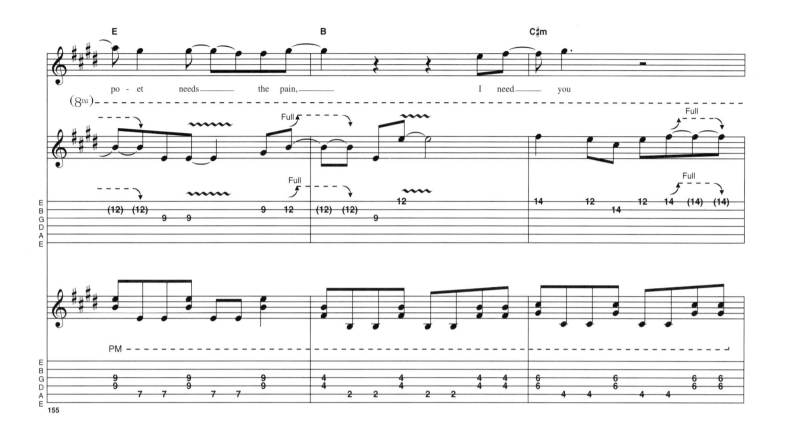

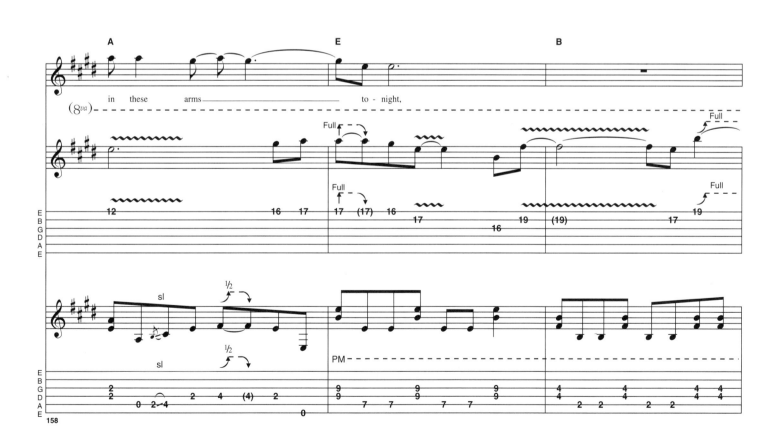

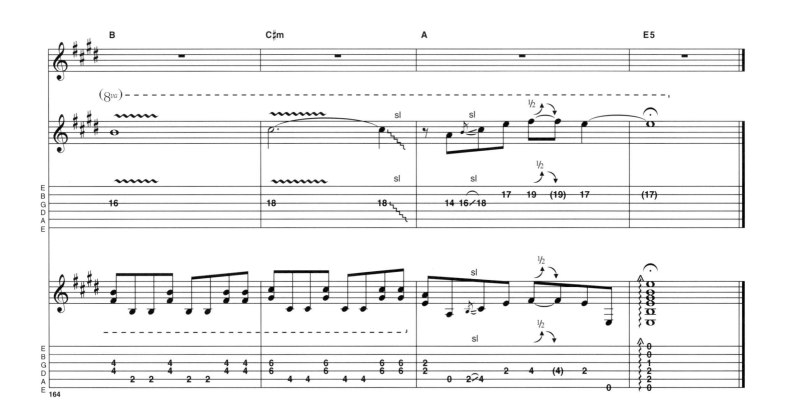

Blaze Of Glory

Words and Music by JON BON JOVI

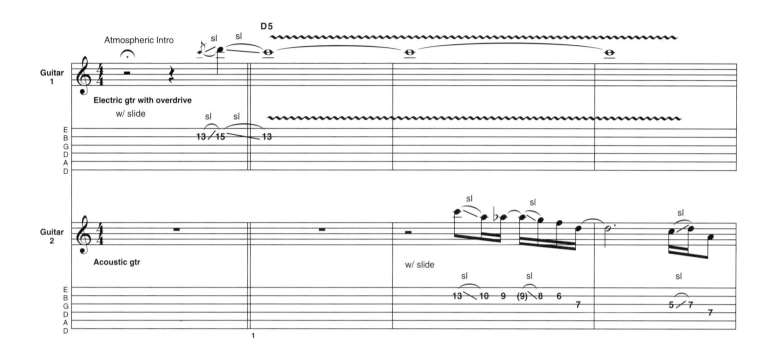

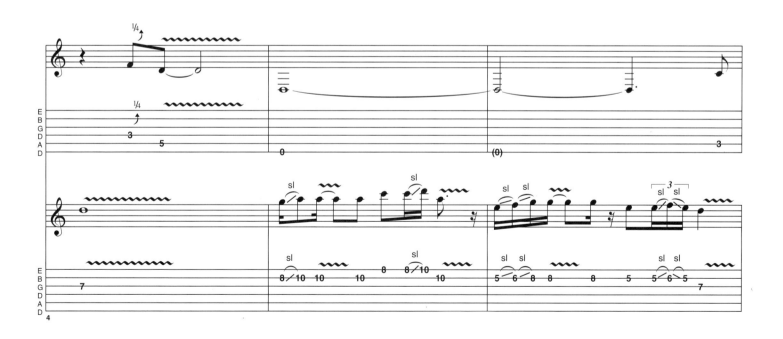

© Copyright 1990 Bon Jovi Publishing/PRI Music Incorporated, USA.
PolyGram International Music Publishing Ltd, 8 St James Square, London SW1.
All Rights Reserved. International Copyright Secured.

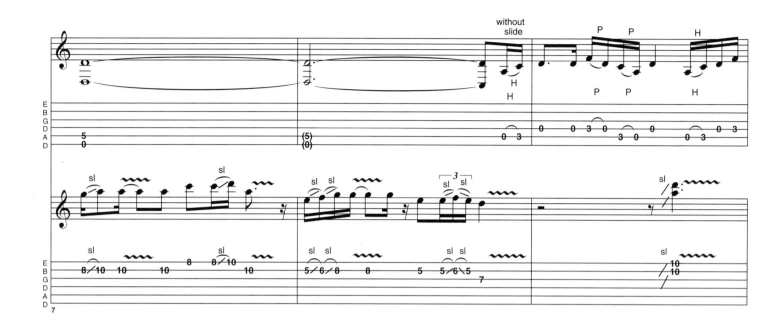

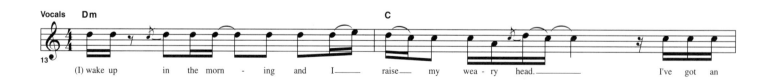

(I) wake up in the morn-ing and I raise my wea-ry head. I've got an

old coat for a pil-low and the earth was last night's bed. I

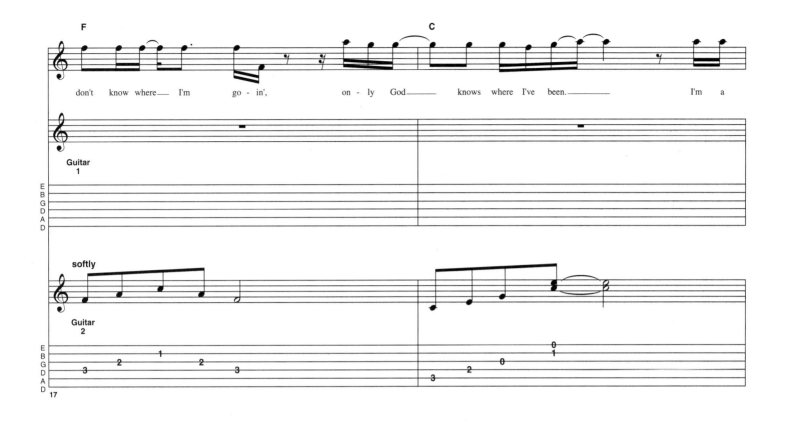

don't know where___ I'm go - in', on - ly God___ knows where I've been.___ I'm a

de - vil on the run, a six gun lo - ver, a can - dle in___ the wind.___ Yeah!

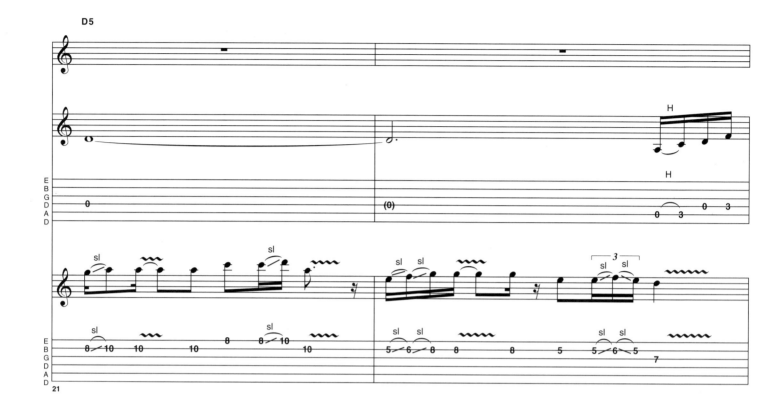

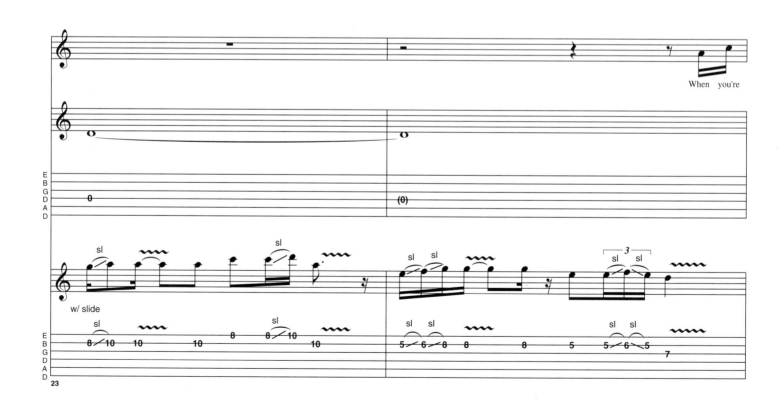

When you're

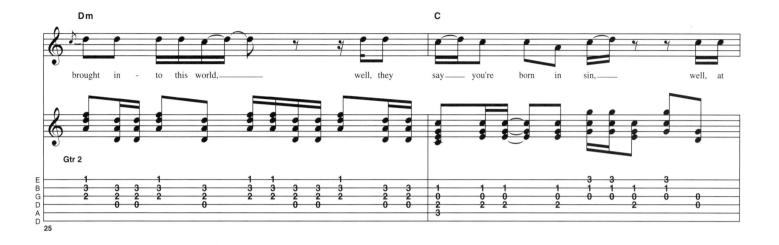

brought in - to this world,_____ well, they say___ you're born in sin,_____ well, at

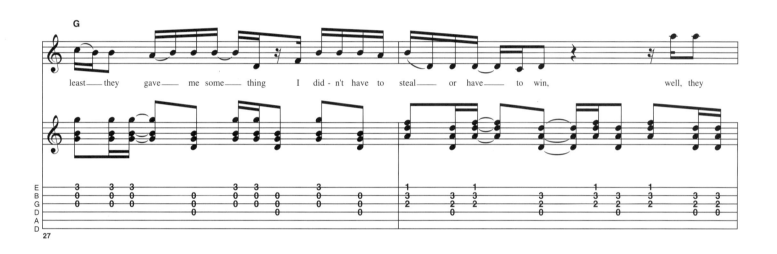

least___ they gave___ me some___ thing I did - n't have to steal___ or have___ to win, well, they

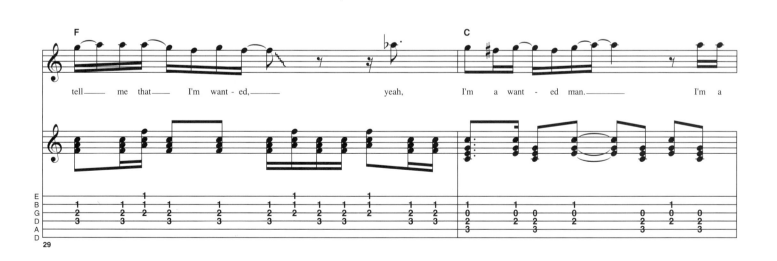

tell___ me that___ I'm want - ed,_____ yeah, I'm a want - ed man._____ I'm a

colt in your sta - ble, I'm what Cain was to A - bel, mis - ter catch me if____ you can. I'm go - in'____

Gtr 1

Gtr 2

31

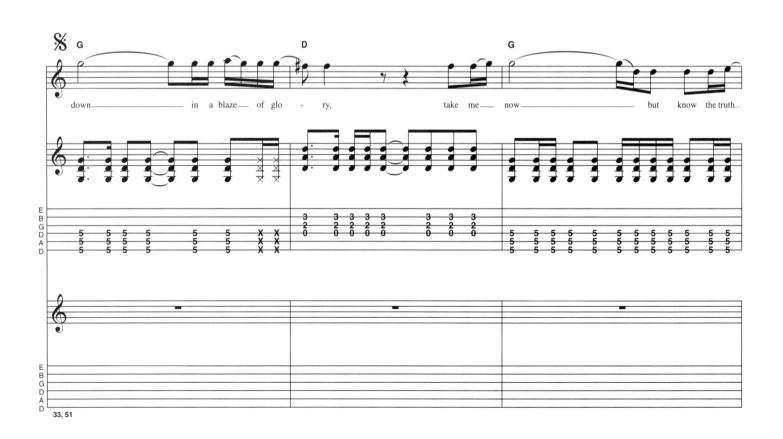

down_____ in a blaze_ of glo - ry, take me_ now_____ but know the truth..

33, 51

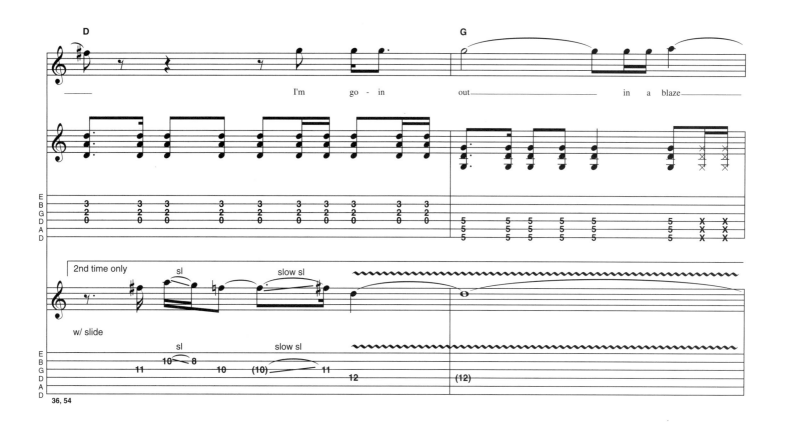

I'm go-in out————————— in a blaze—————

2nd time only

w/ slide

36, 54

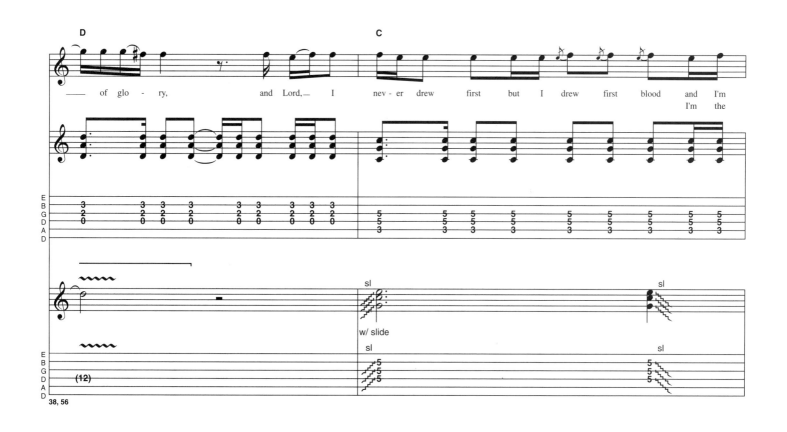

————— of glo-ry, and Lord,— I nev-er drew first but I drew first blood and I'm I'm the

w/ slide

38, 56

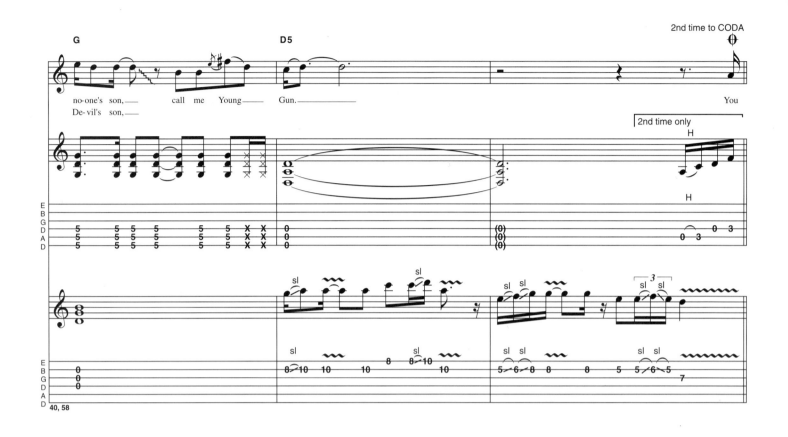

no-one's son,— call me Young—— Gun.——— You
De- vil's son,—

ask a-bout— my con - science and I of - fer you— my soul. You ask if I'll grow— to be— a wise— man when I

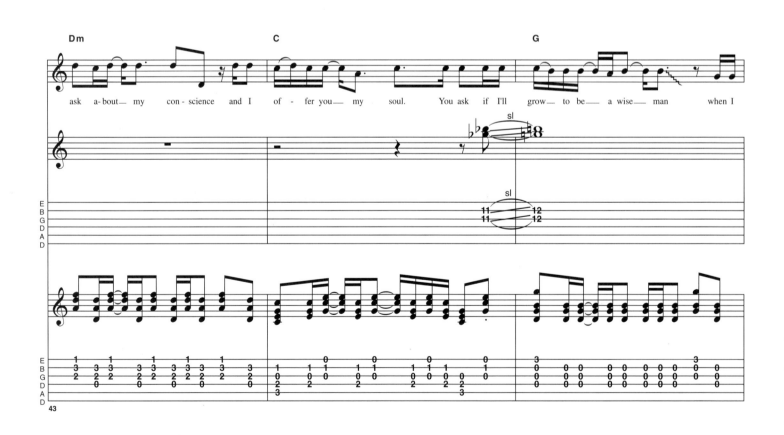

ask if I'll——— grow old. You ask me if——— I'd known love and what it's like to

sing songs in the rain,——— well, I've seen love come, I've seen it shot——— down, I've seen it die——— in vain. Shot

D.S. al CODA

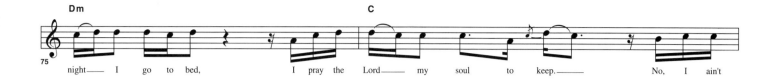

night____ I go to bed, I pray the Lord____ my soul to keep.____ No, I ain't

look - 'in for____ for - give - ness but be - fore I'm six foot deep Lord

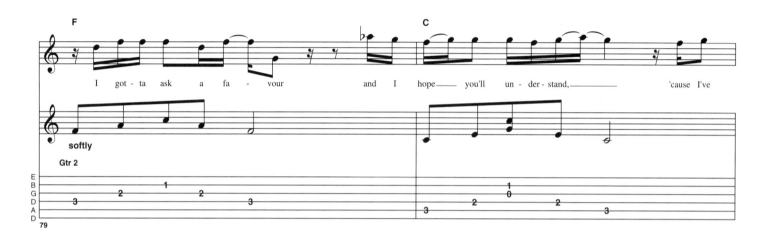

I got - ta ask a fa - vour and I hope____ you'll un - der - stand,____ 'cause I've

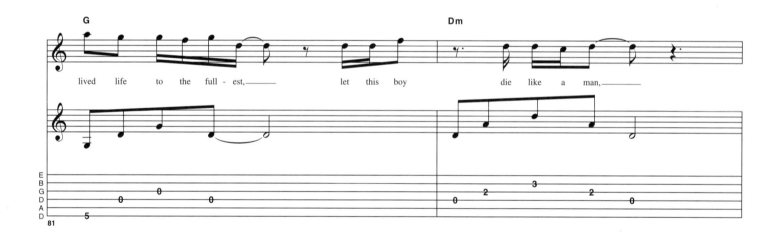

lived life to the full - est,____ let this boy die like a man,____

star - in' down____ a bul - let, let me make____ my fi - nal____ stand. Shot

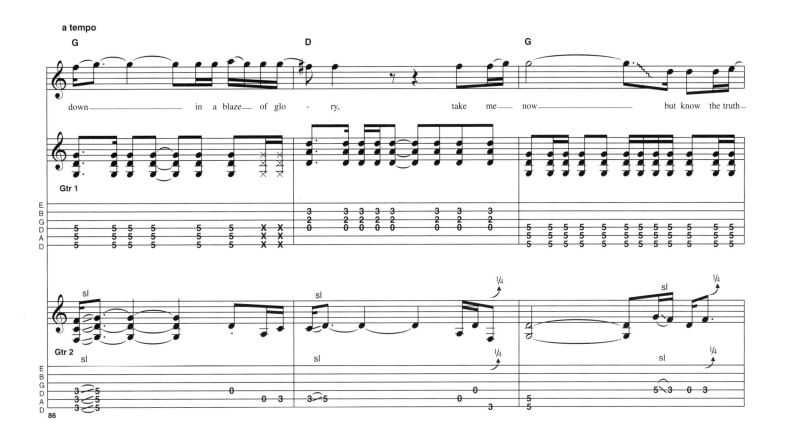

down_____ in a blaze___ of glo - ry,   take me___ now_____ but know the truth___

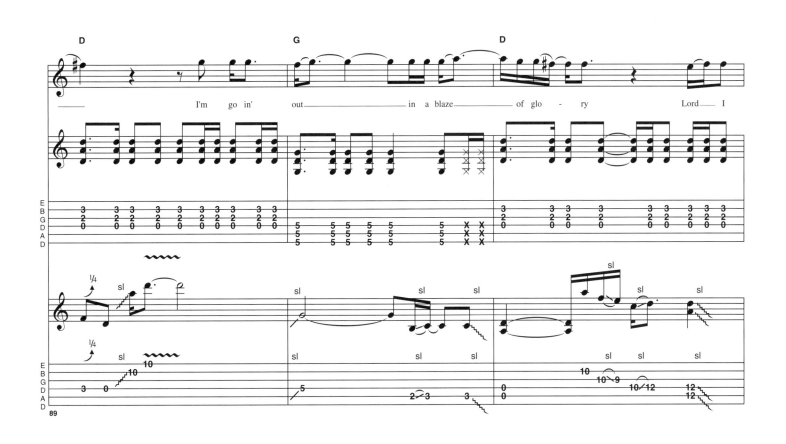

_____ I'm go in' out_____ in a blaze_____ of glo - ry   Lord___ I

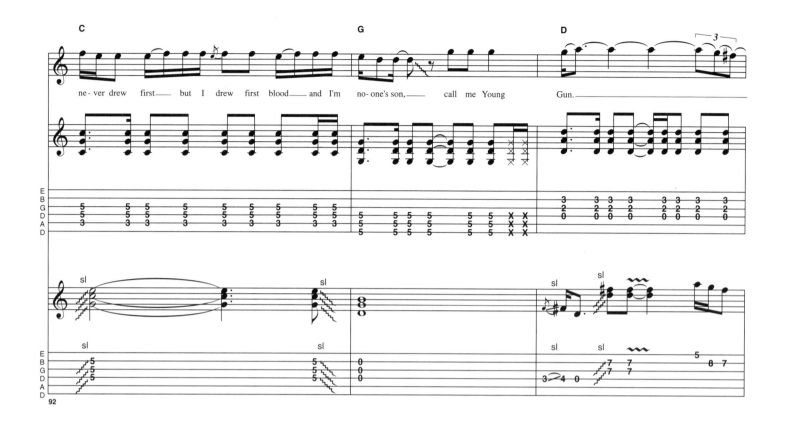

ne- ver drew first —— but I drew first blood —— and I'm no- one's son, —— call me Young Gun. ——

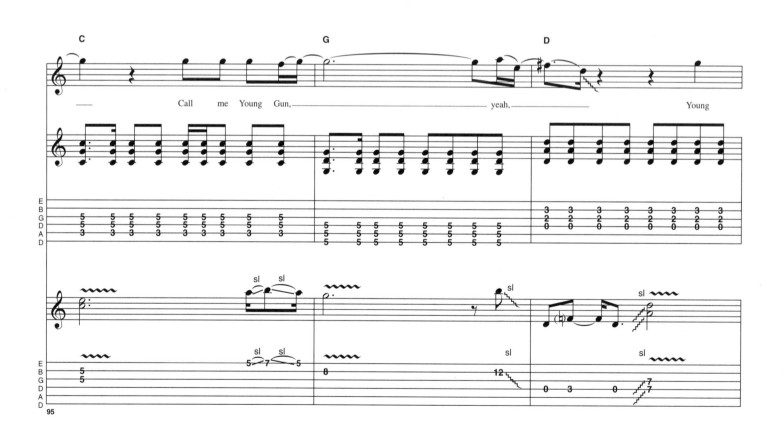

—— Call me Young Gun, ———————————————— yeah, ——————— Young

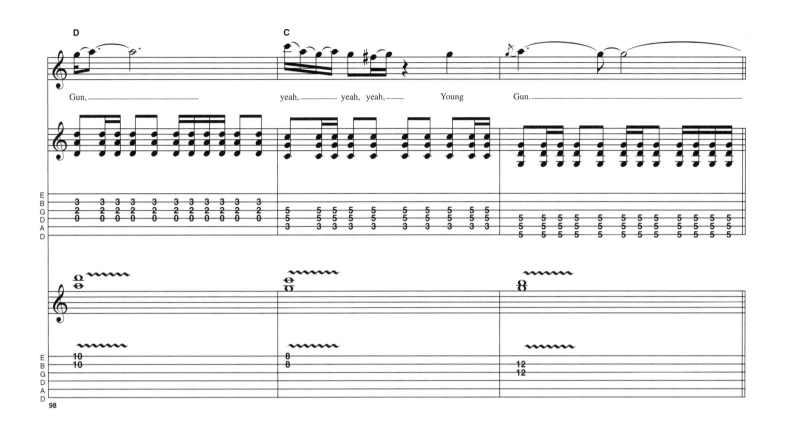

Gun,———————— yeah,———— yeah, yeah,———— Young Gun.————————

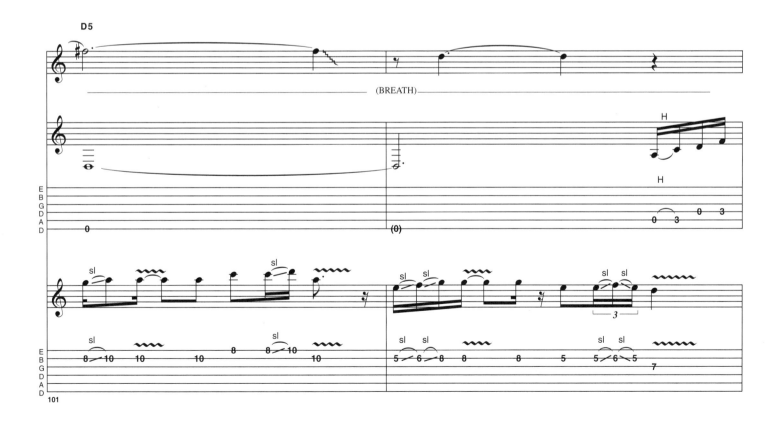

(BREATH)————————

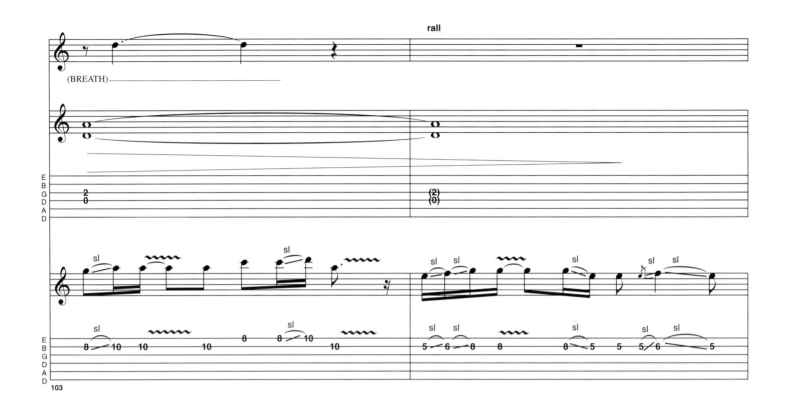

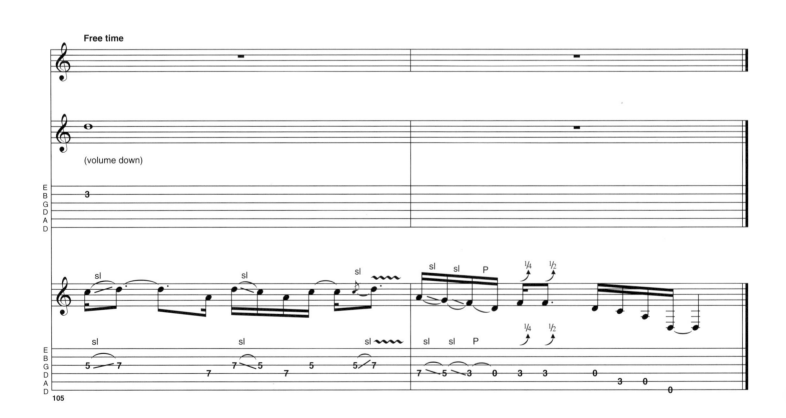

Keep The Faith

Words and Music by JON BON JOVI,
RICHIE SAMBORA and DESMOND CHILD

© Copyright 1992 PolyGram International Music Publishing Incorporated/Bon Jovi Publishing/Aggressive
Music/EMI April Music Incorporated//Desmobile Music Company, USA. EMI Songs Limited, 127 Charing Cross Road,
London WC2 (33.33%)/Polygram Music Publishing Ltd, 47 British Grove, London W4 (66.66%) .
All Rights Reserved. International Copyright Secured.

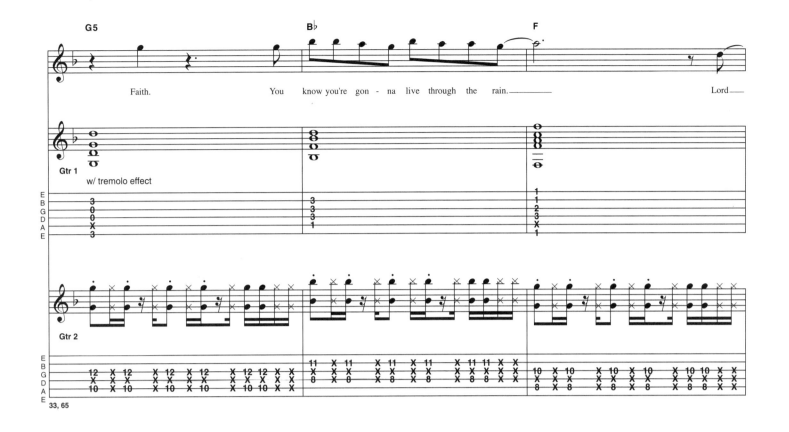

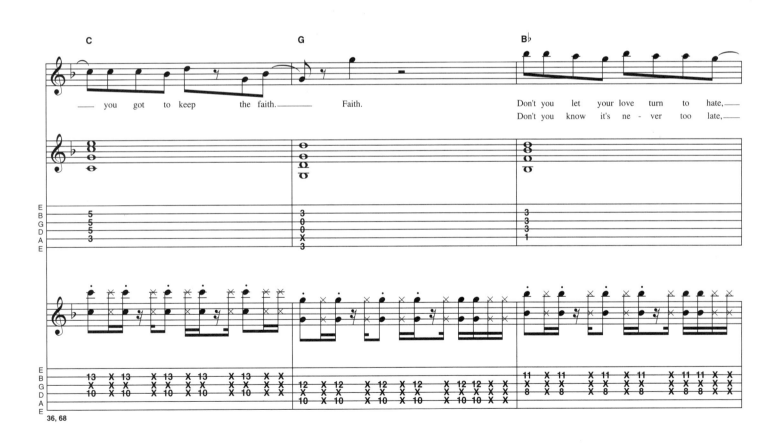

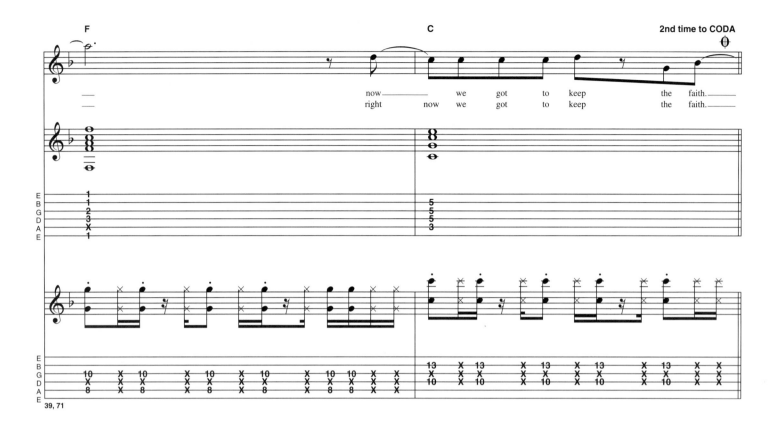

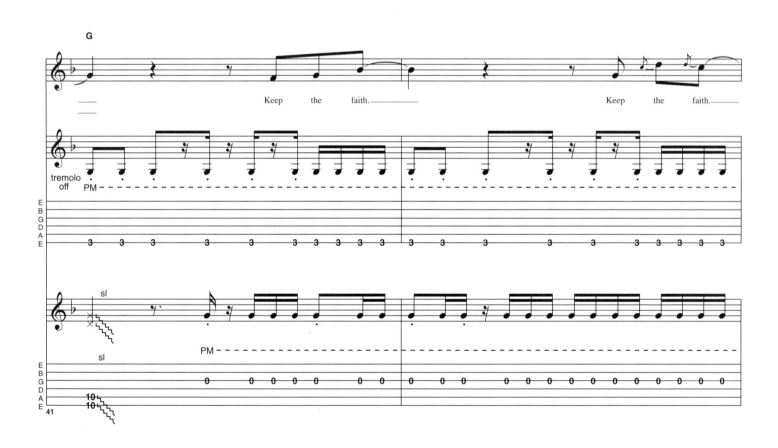

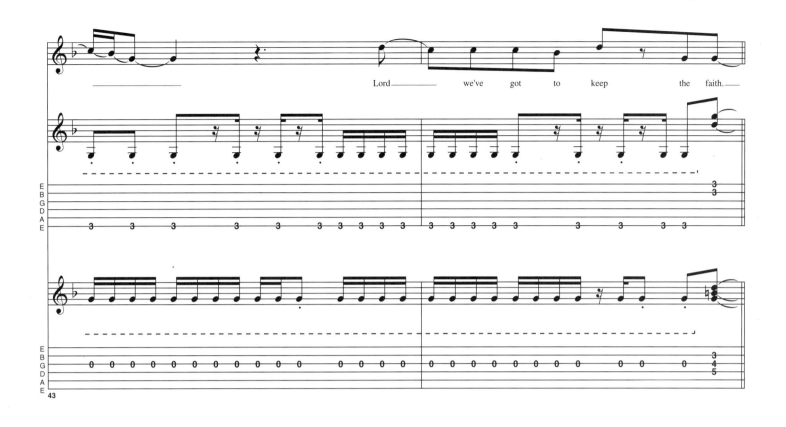

Lord———— we've got to keep the faith.——

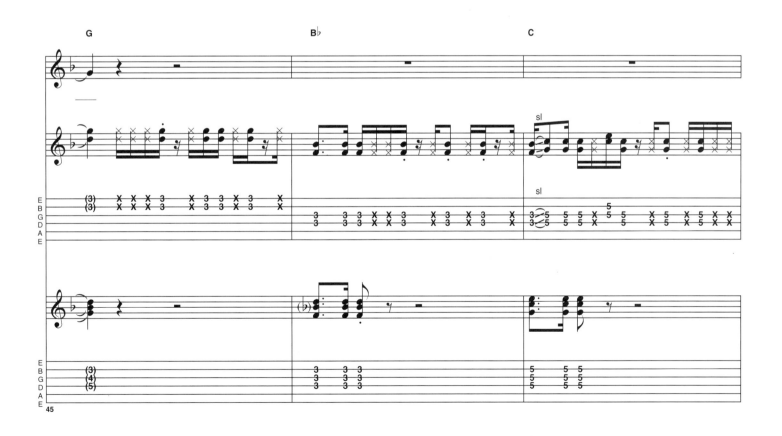

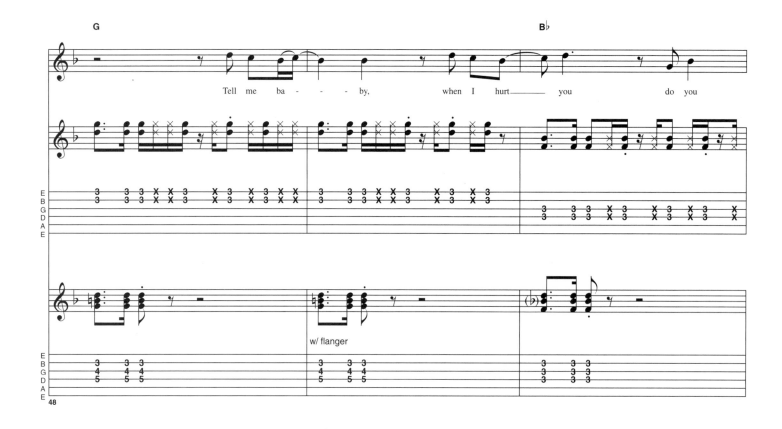

Tell me ba - - by, when I hurt you do you

w/ flanger

48

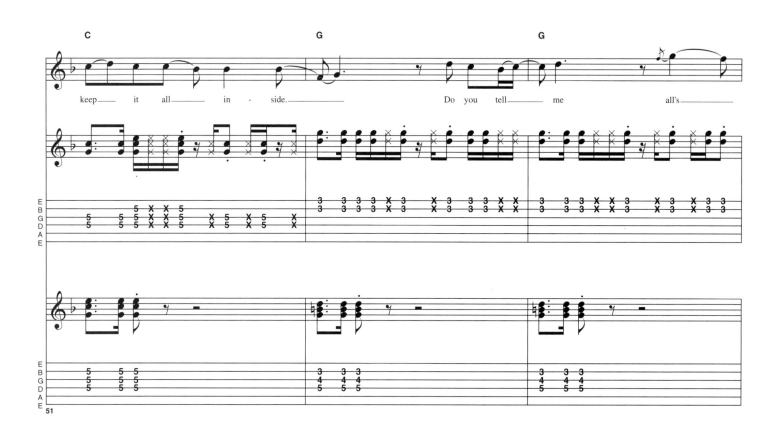

keep it all in - side. Do you tell me all's

51

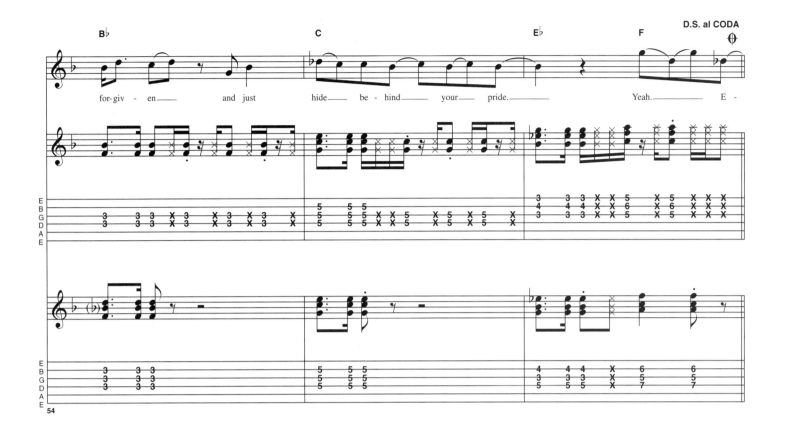

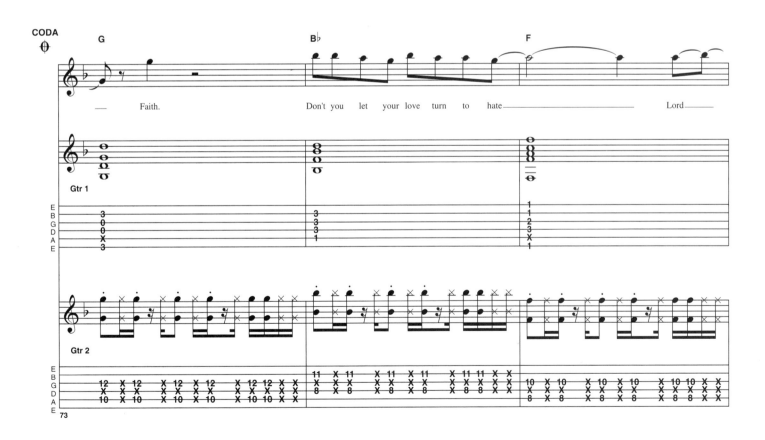

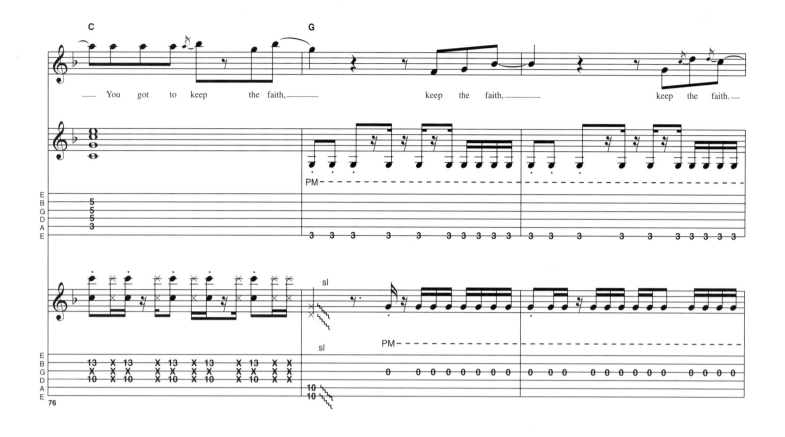

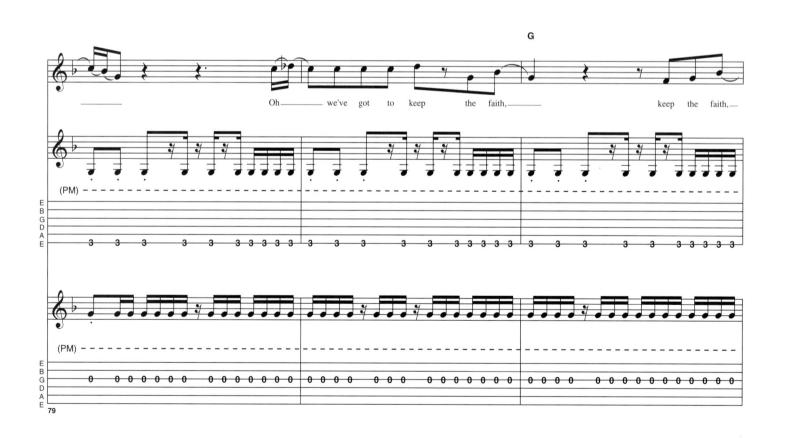

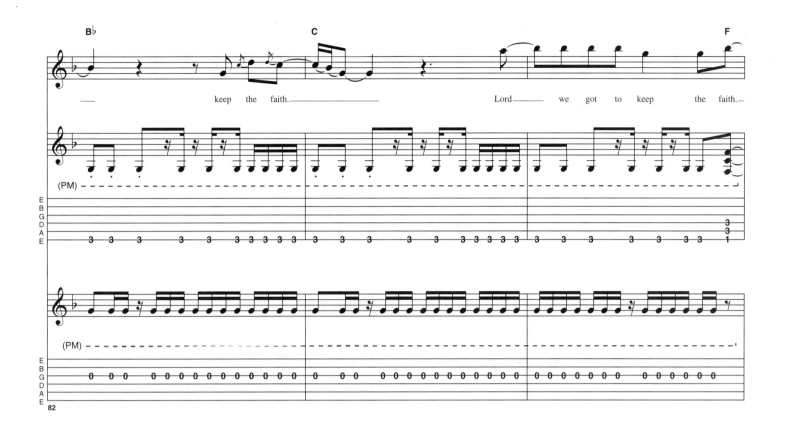

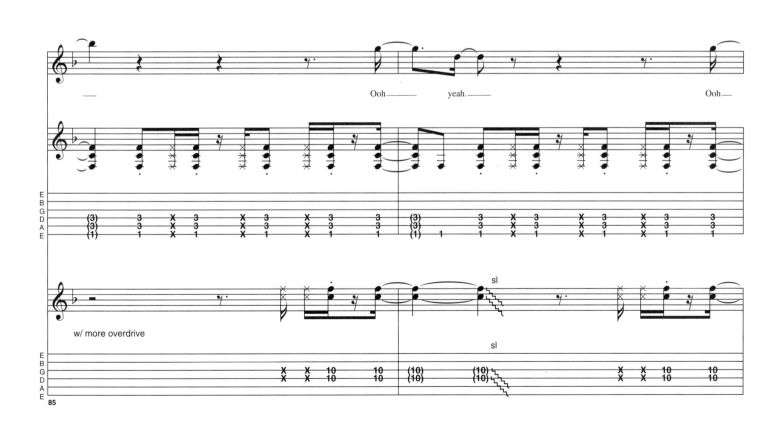

yeah,   yeah,   yeah.

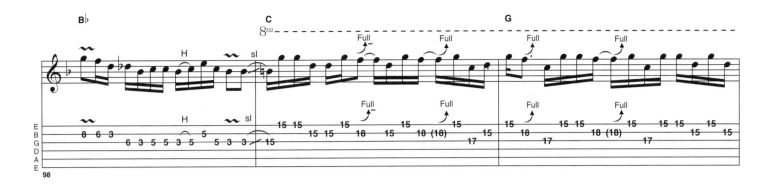

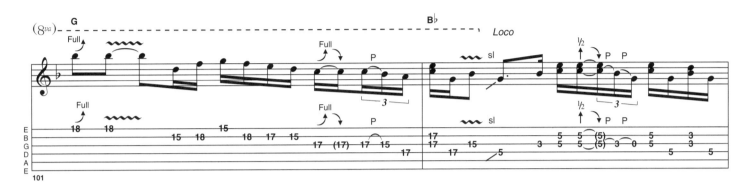

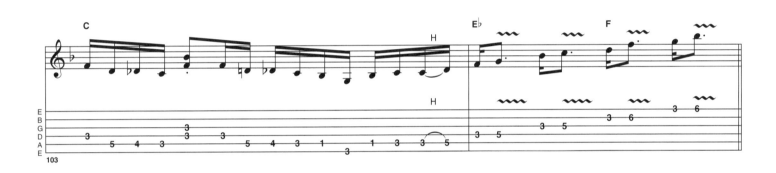

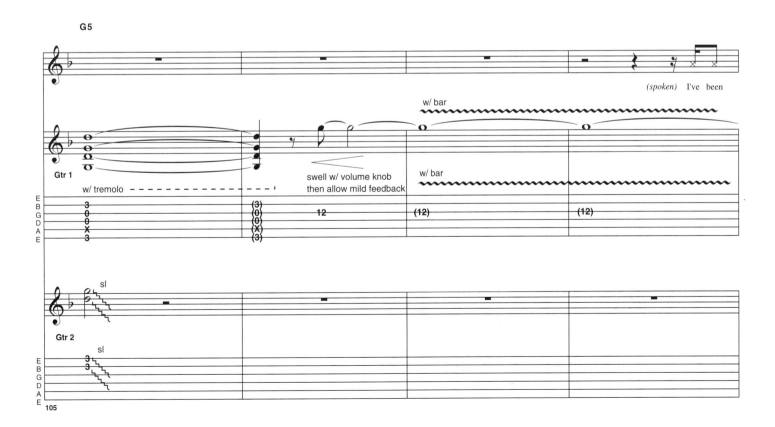

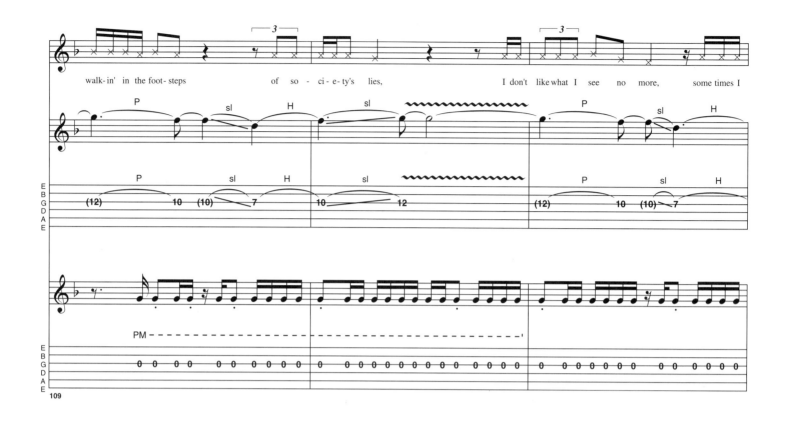

walk-in' in the foot-steps   of so - ci - e- ty's lies,   I don't like what I see   no   more,   some times I

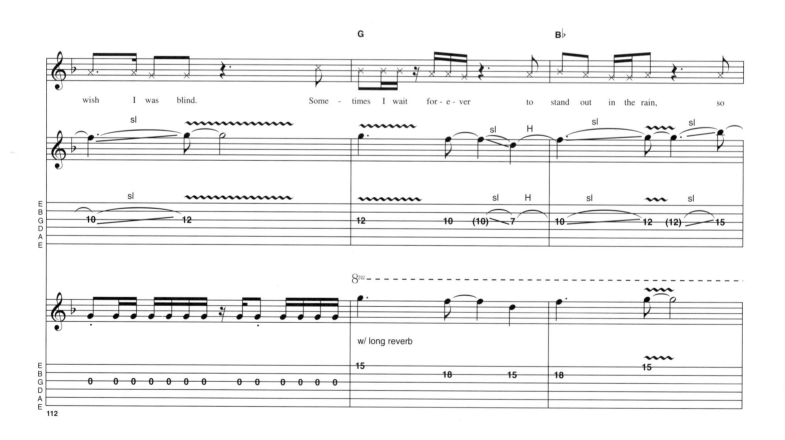

wish   I was blind.   Some - times I wait for- e - ver   to stand out   in the rain,   so

w/ long reverb

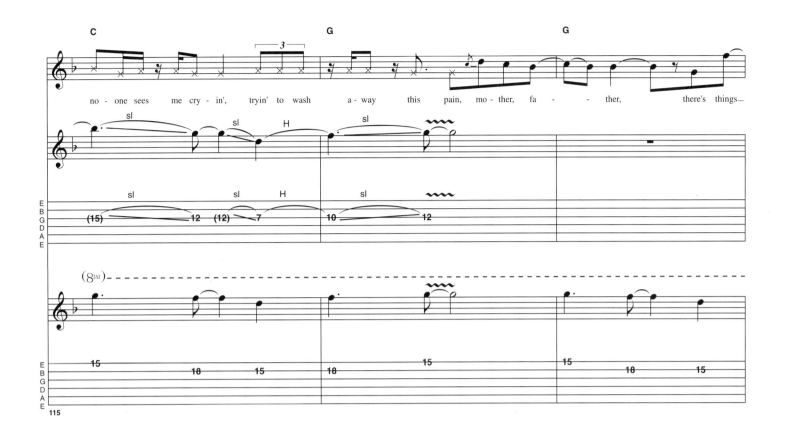

no - one sees me cry - in', tryin' to wash a - way this pain, mo - ther, fa - - ther, there's things

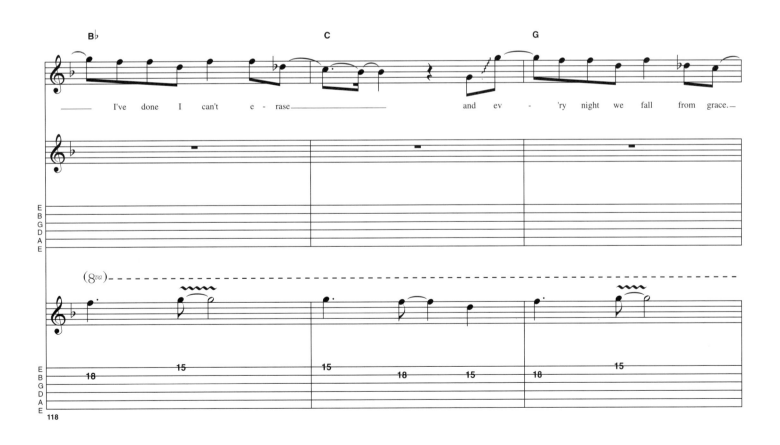

I've done I can't e - rase and ev - 'ry night we fall from grace.

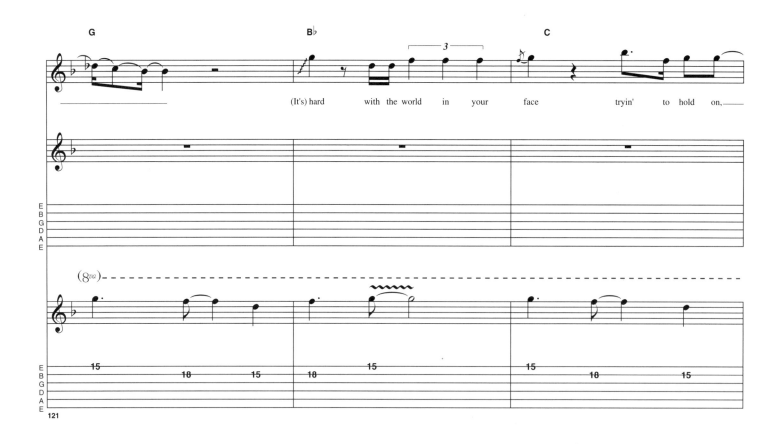

(It's) hard with the world in your face tryin' to hold on,

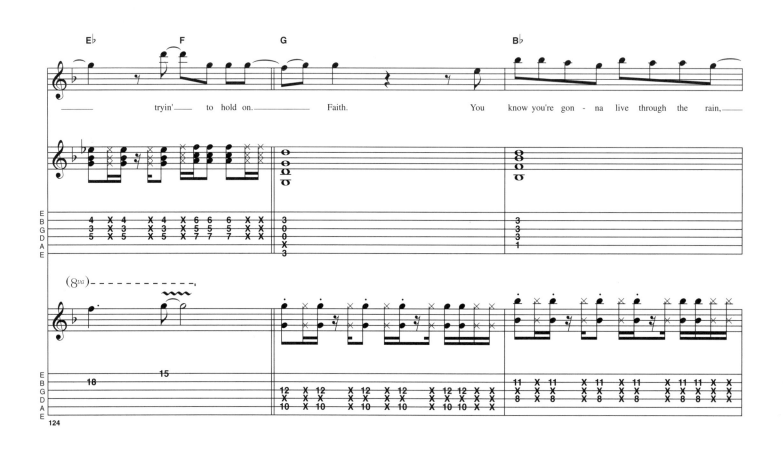

tryin' to hold on. Faith. You know you're gon-na live through the rain,

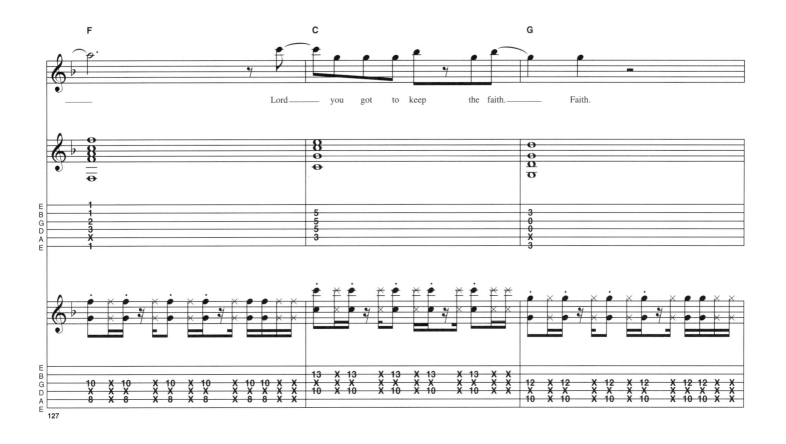

Lord____ you got to keep the faith.____ Faith.

127

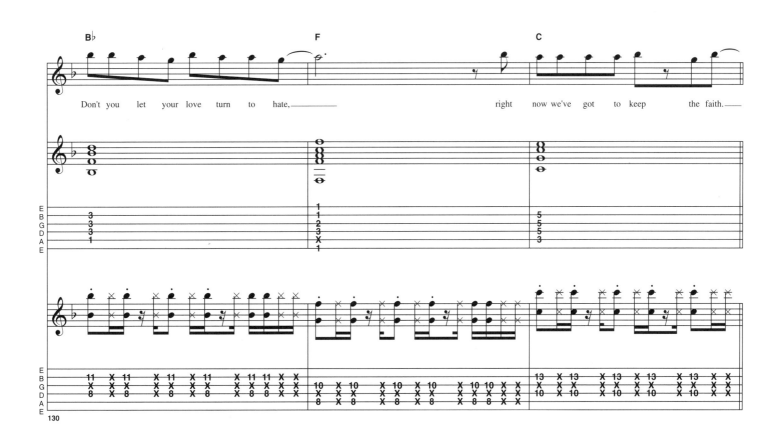

Don't you let your love turn to hate,____ right now we've got to keep the faith.____

130

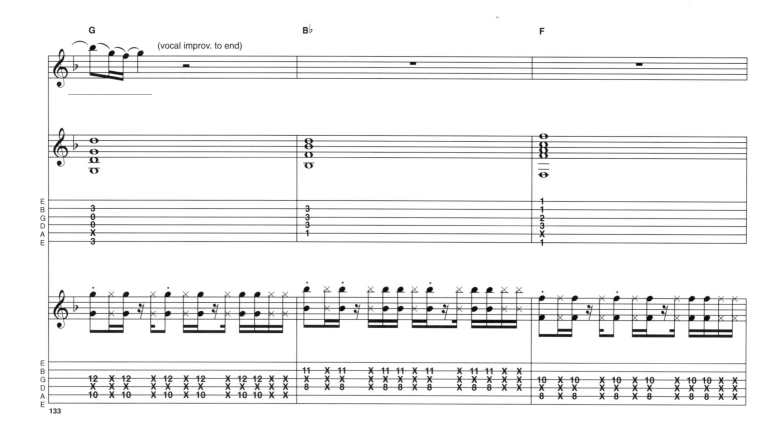

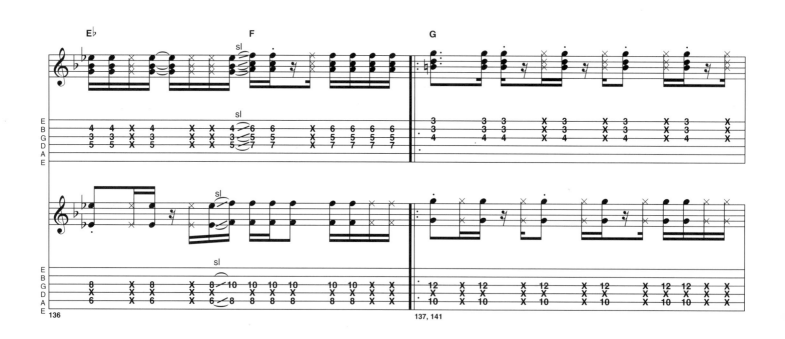

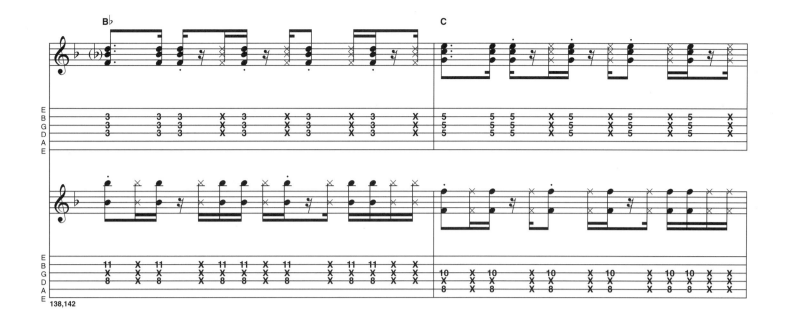

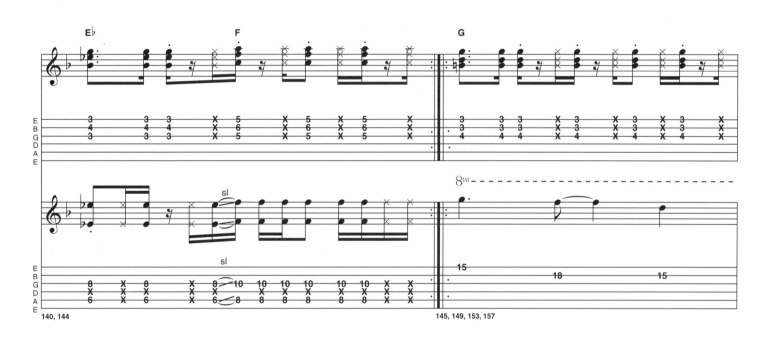

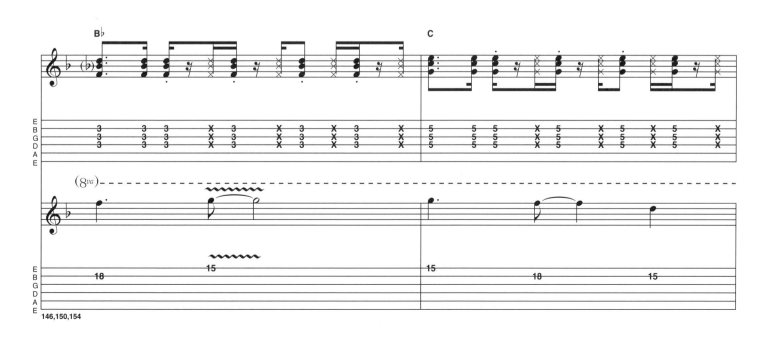

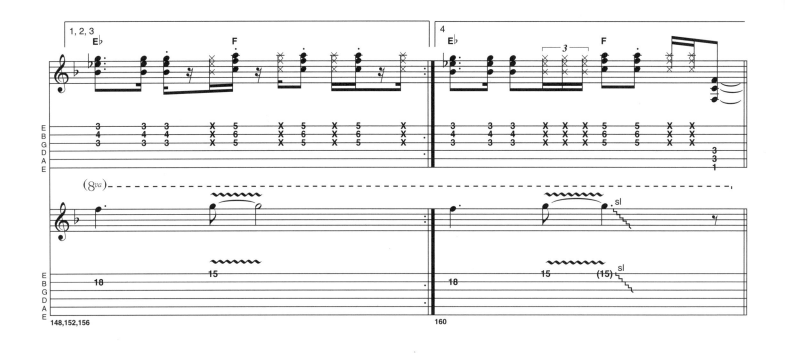

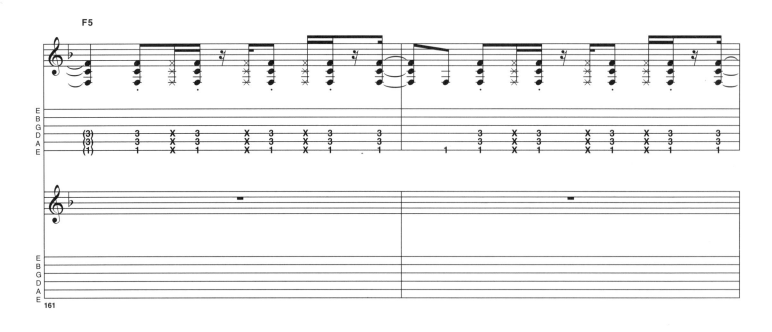

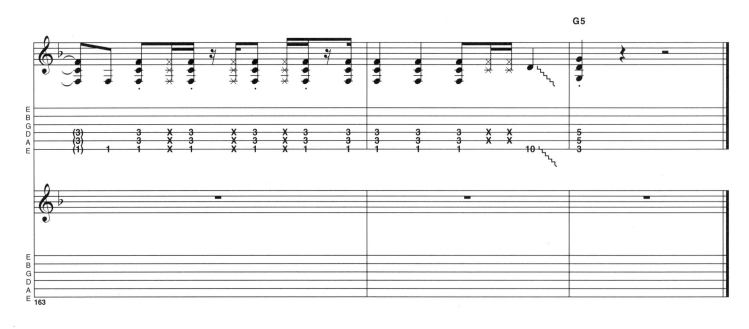

Bad Medicine

Words and Music by JON BON JOVI,
RICHIE SAMBORA and DESMOND CHILD

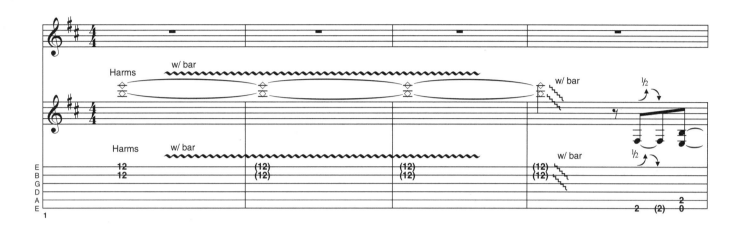

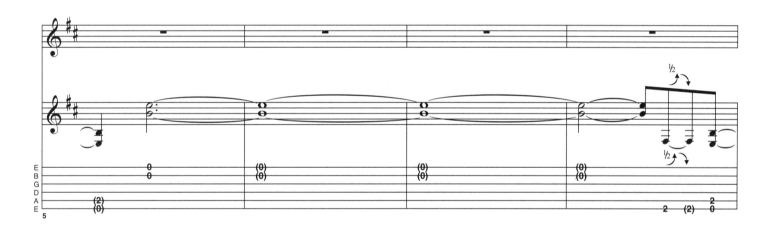

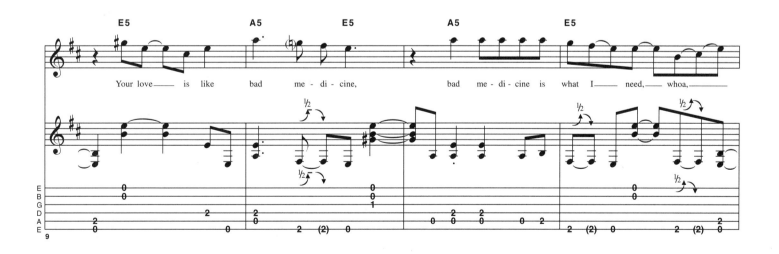

© Copyright 1988 Bon Jovi Publishing/New Jersey Underground Music Incorporated/Desmobile Music, USA.
Polygram Music Publishing Ltd, 47 British Grove, London W4 (66.66%)/EMI Songs Limited,
127 Charing Cross Road, London WC2 (33.33%).
All Rights Reserved. International Copyright Secured.

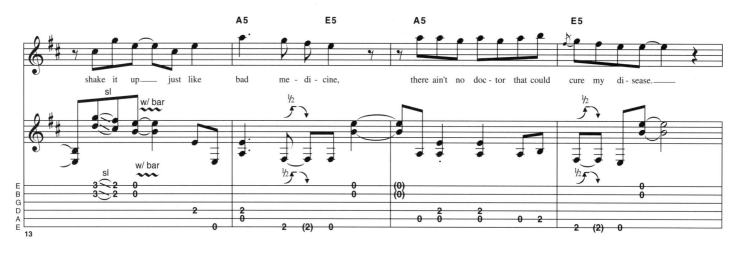

shake it up——— just like bad me - di - cine, there ain't no doc - tor that could cure my di - sease.———

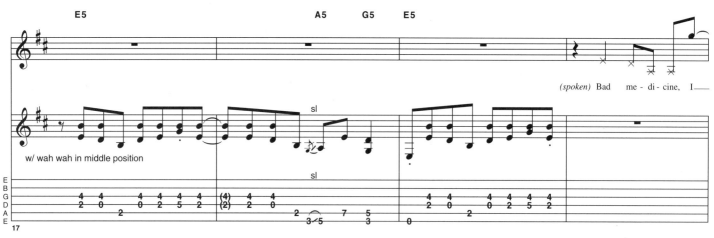

(spoken) Bad me - di - cine, I———

w/ wah wah in middle position

——— got a fe - ver, got a per - ma - nent dis - ease and it - 'll take more than a doc - tor to pre - scribe a re - me - dy. I
don't need no nee - dle to be gi - vin' me a thrill and I don't need no an - aes - the - sia or a nurse to bring a pill. I got a

(2nd time only)
w/ wah

——— got lots of mo - ney but it is - n't what I need, gon - na take more than a shot to get the poi - son out——— of me. And
dir - ty down add - ict - ion that does - n't leave a track, I got a jolt for your af - fec - tion like a mon - key on my back. There

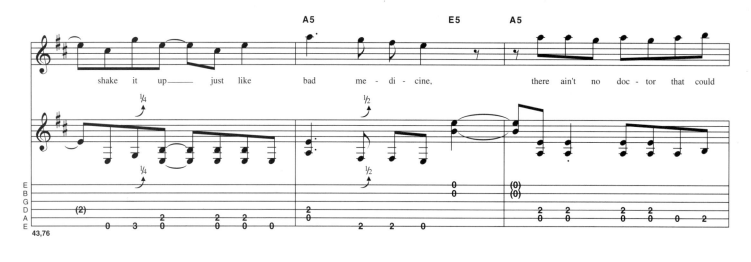

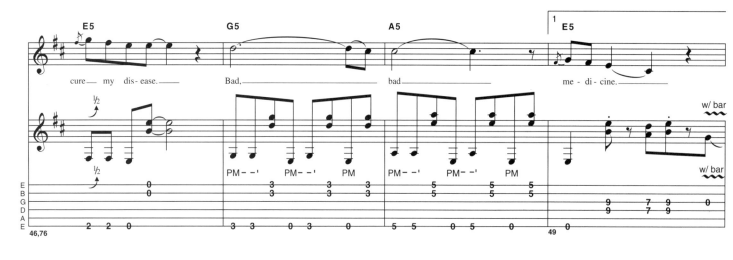

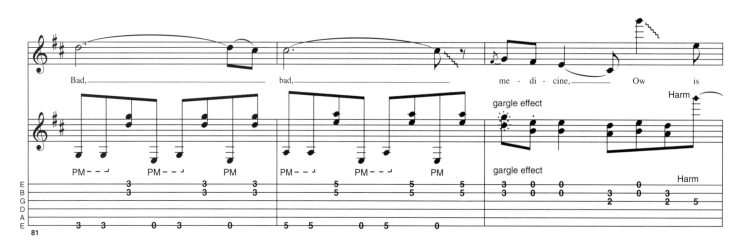

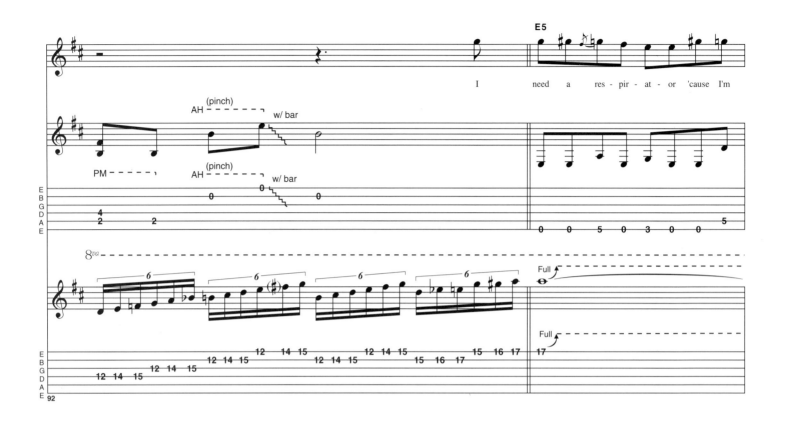

I need a res - pir - at - or 'cause I'm

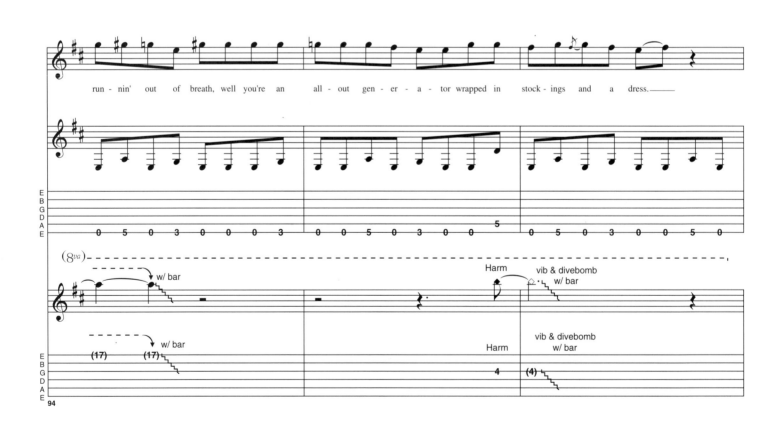

run - nin' out of breath, well you're an all - out gen - er - a - tor wrapped in stock - ings and a dress.

When you find your med - ic - ine you'll take what you can get, 'cause if there's

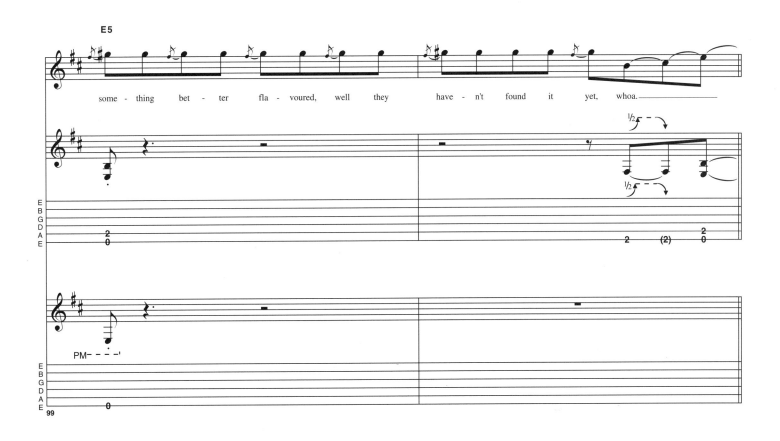

some - thing bet - ter fla - voured, well they have - n't found it yet, whoa.

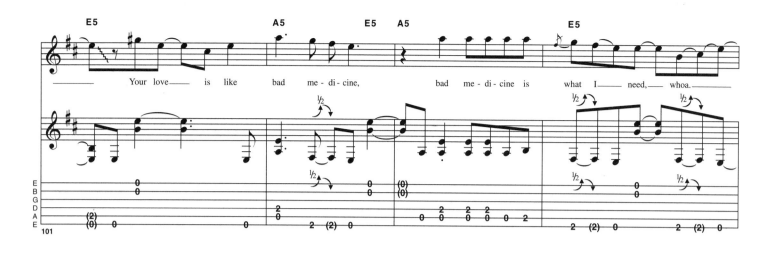

Your love——— is like bad me-di-cine, bad me-di-cine is what I——— need, whoa.———

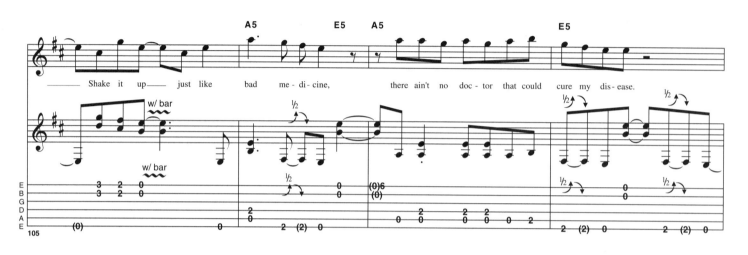

——— Shake it up——— just like bad me-di-cine, there ain't no doc-tor that could cure my dis-ease.

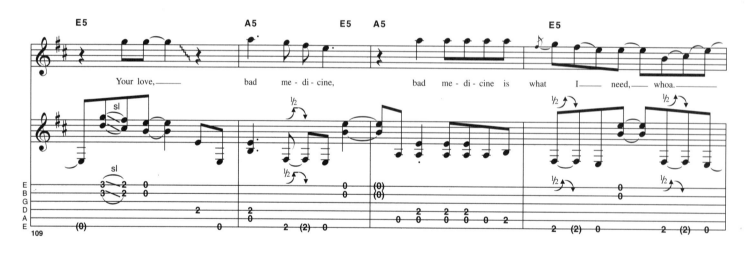

Your love,——— bad me-di-cine, bad me-di-cine is what I——— need,——— whoa.

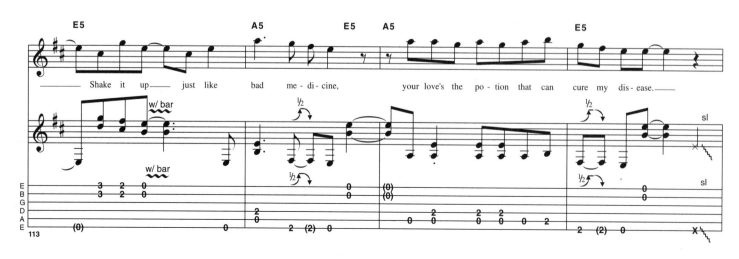

——— Shake it up——— just like bad me-di-cine, your love's the po-tion that can cure my dis-ease.

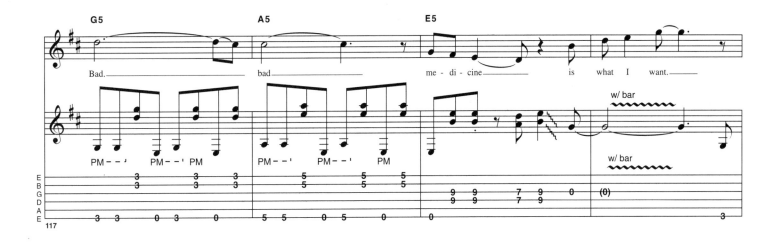

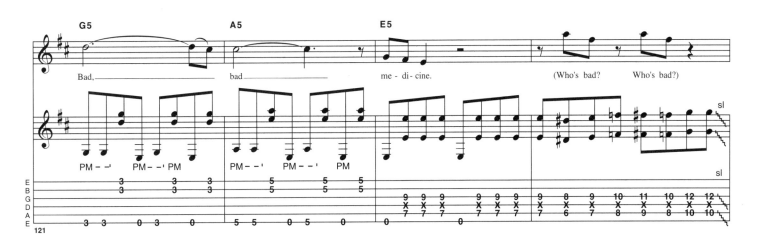

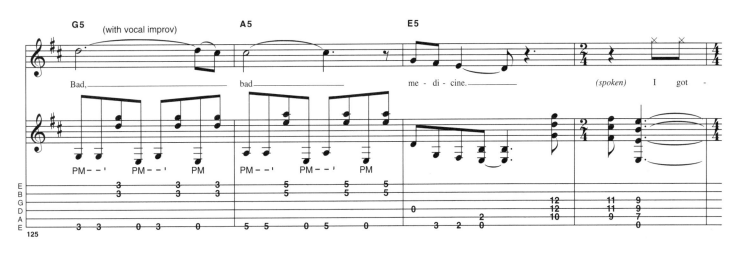

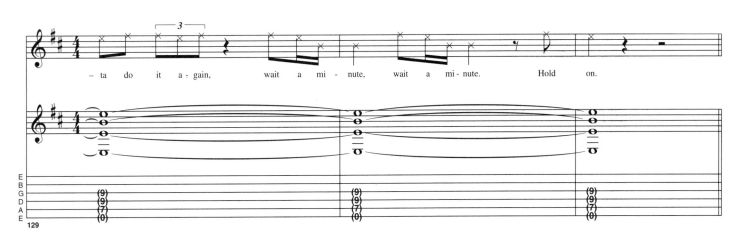

I'm not done, one more time with feel-ing, come on.

Al-right, help me out now.

Your love___ is like bad me-di-cine, bad me-di-cine is what I___ need,___ whoa.

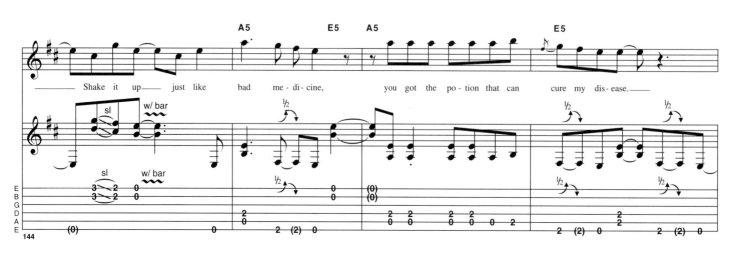

___ Shake it up ___ just like bad me-di-cine, you got the po-tion that can cure my dis-ease.___

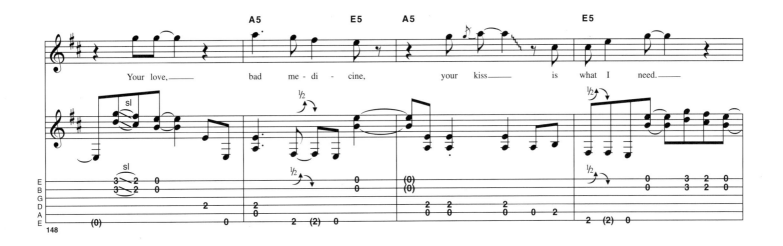

Your love,_____ bad me - di - cine, your kiss_____ is what I need._____

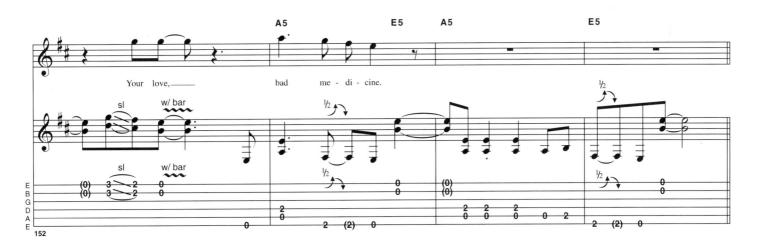

Your love,_____ bad me - di - cine.

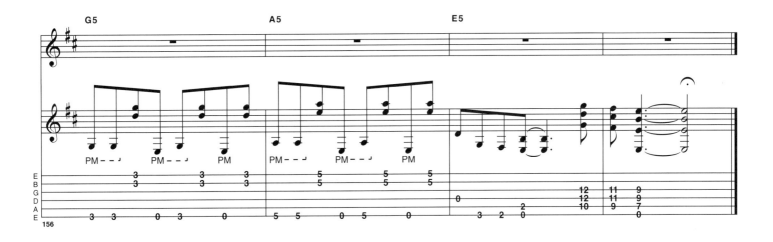

play guitar with...

the beatles
day tripper
dear prudence
get back
i feel fine
norwegian wood
paperback writer
sgt. pepper's lonely
  hearts club band
yesterday
Order No. NO90665

blur
country house
end of a century
girls and boys
mr. robinson's quango
parklife
stereotypes
the universal
tracy jacks
Order No. AM935320

bon jovi
in and out of love
in these arms
lay your hands on me
livin' on a prayer
never say goodbye
wanted dead or alive
you give love a bad name
Order No. AM92558

eric clapton
bad love
i shot the sheriff
layla
let it grow
sunshine of your love
tears in heaven
white room
wonderful tonight
Order No. AM950862

phil collins
another day in paradise
don't lose my number
i don't wanna know
i wish it would rain down
inside out
one more night
thunder & lightning
Order No. AM928147

the cranberries
dreams
hollywood
how
i can't be with you
ridiculous thoughts
still can't recognise the way i feel
when you're gone
zombie
Order No. AM941699

buddy holly
heartbeat
oh boy
rave on
that'll be the day
words of love
peggy sue
Order No. AM943734

kula shaker
govinda
hey dude
hush
into the deep
knight on the town
smart dogs
tattva
Order No. AM943767

john lennon
cold turkey
come together
happy xmas (war is over)
help!
i want you (she's so heavy)
woman
Order No. AM943756

bob marley
buffalo soldier
could you be loved
exodus
i shot the sheriff
jamming
no woman, no cry
waiting in vain
Order No. AM937739

metallica
ain't my bitch
enter sandman
fade to black
nothing else matters
the unforgiven
welcome home (sanitarium)
Order No. AM92559

alanis morissette
all i really want
hand in my pocket
ironic
mary jane
not the doctor
perfect
you learn
you oughta know
Order No. AM943723

oasis
cigarettes & alcohol
hey now
morning glory
roll with it
she's electric
supersonic
up in the sky
Order No. AM935330

ocean colour scene
the circle
the day we caught the train
fleeting mind
40 past midnight
policemen and pirates
the riverboat song
you've got it bad
Order No. AM943712

elvis presley
all shook up
blue suede shoes
his latest flame (marie's the name)
hound dog
jailhouse rock
king creole
lawdy miss clawdy
my baby left me
Order No. AM937090

pulp
babies
common people
disco 2000
do you remember the first time?
mis-shapes
something changed
sorted for e's & wizz
Order No. AM938124

the rolling stones
brown sugar
get off of my cloud
gimme shelter
honky tonk women
(i can't get no) satisfaction
jumpin' jack flash
19th nervous breakdown
paint it black
Order No. AM90247

sting
an englishman in new york
fields of gold
fragile
if you love somebody set them free
moon over bourbon street
straight to my heart
they dance alone
Order No. AM928092

the stone roses
elephant stone
i am the resurrection
i wanna be adored
made of stone
she bangs the drums
ten storey love song
waterfall
Order No. AM943701

paul weller
the changingman
into tomorrow
out of the sinking
stanley road
sunflower
wild wood
woodcutter's son
you do something to me
Order No. AM937827